PEPPER

Graphic design and artwork:

Distributed in 2016 by Abrams, an imprint of Abrams
© 2016 Published by Editions de La Martinière, an imprint of EDLM

ISBN: 978 1 4197 2932 4

Color separation: Turquoise
Printing in April 2017 in Portugal
10 9 8 7 6 5 4 3 2 1

PEPPER

AUTHORS
ERWANN DE KERROS
BÉNÉDICTE BORTOLI

WITH THE COLLABORATION OF
THIERRY NÉRISSON
MARC JEANSON

PHOTOGRAPHY
OF PEPPER AND RECIPES
GUILLAUME CZERW

ABRAMS | NEW YORK

« Le sel de l'existence est essentiellement dans le poivre qu'on y met. »

ALPHONSE ALLAIS

« Être homme, c'est précisément être responsable. (…)
C'est sentir, en posant sa pierre, que l'on contribue à bâtir le monde. »

ANTOINE DE SAINT-EXUPÉRY

Technical terms and abbreviations marked with an asterisk are
explained in the glossary on page 290.

Opposite:
Timiz pepper flower, Ethiopia.

CONTENTS

THE
"PEPPER FERRYMAN"

Pepper around the world. This Earth of ours with its many lands, some discovered, some yet to discover, opening up to human cultures and the knowledge that comes from the land... and the pepper — my chosen spice — individual peppercorns and all kinds of pepper, which are the starting points and the core of the adventure that has occupied Terre Exotique for the past twenty years. Penja is where I discovered pepper, the land that introduced me to the little seed* that was the beginning of everything in 1992. I had finished my business studies and was preparing for military service when my destiny was rather shaken up by a badly broken foot, an accident while I was traveling in Asia. So here I was in new circumstances and without any particular objective to pursue. I then had the idea to go abroad for a year with my future wife Marie. By luck and with the help of certain contacts, I ended up in Penja, a community in the northwest of Cameroon, excited by the prospect of managing a little 100-hectare "mixed" plantation. A pretty silly project when you consider my complete lack of experience. I had a green thumb but that was all! The land belonged to a French lawyer, Mr. Aubriet, who had bought it long before I got there. For twenty years, young students and apprentices of all kinds had been coming here for one or two seasons at most. There was a wooden stilt house with a terrace attached that gave a superb view across the whole Penja valley. There was a spring and a dam, and six or seven horses retired from the Douala riding club that I would ride across the plantation. It was a life that combined necessity with pleasure, and sometimes some extraordinary experiences. A basic existence, without electricity or running water, with a generator that did from time to time delight us by not breaking down. If we were careful, we sometimes enjoyed an air-conditioned siesta, sometimes a little illumination in the evening.

It was in this rustic and enchanting milieu that, day by day, month by month, I acquired an understanding of the subtleties of pepper cultivation, partly learned from the locals and partly by reading certain rare works on the subject written in English. I was told when I got there that my job was to make sure that "things went well"... a huge and vague brief that was open to any possibility. So I improvised a pretty experimental style of management, enlivened by shared moments beyond the boundaries of the plantation, like setting up the Penja football team and, on the more serious side, the strikes with a certain amount of attendant violence. All relationships were ruled by a great spirit of spontaneity.

The pepper plants were spread across more than twenty-nine hectares, which at that time made the Aubriet plantation the largest in Cameroon. Armed with bulldozers and with no second thoughts, we ripped up decades-old lianas to plant the more productive and very profitable bananas. Before my arrival, the plantation was selling at most half a container of pepper and we were far from any plan to export it. Penja pepper is traded locally as a commonplace spice. I do all the same remember Mr. Aubriet telling me with a twinkle in his eye: "Erwann, Penja pepper is the best in the world. That's not just me; it's the people who say so." In those years, these little grey seeds had already attracted a following of enthusiasts despite their insignificant production compared with the large-scale output of bananas, pineapples and papayas. And given its minimal value on the market — 900 Central African francs per kilo at best (before devaluation) — the business was struggling to survive. That it did survive was essentially due to rising prices in the local market. Even so, we were far from any expectation of a PGI* or some other form of recognition. After four years watching and

Tending a young plantation of pepper,
Piper nigrum, in Penja, Cameroon.

working at the heart of this plantation, it was time for me to return to France. But this unique experience left a lasting mark on me, in both human and professional terms. So a year later, I started my own import business, Terre Exotique, wholly devoted to the import of exotic fruits. Mostly what I brought into Europe were pineapples, a fruit that I had planted in the Penja valley in some quantity (around 600,000 plants, some ten hectares). With each shipment, I did regularly manage to slip in some white Penja pepper that I passed on to friends and acquaintances, enthusiasts and professionals. Professionals always said the same thing: yes, this was exceptional pepper, but it was much too expensive for the market. When we spoke of the particular qualities of Penja pepper, we linked it to the concepts of origin and 'cru' – concepts already established in the worlds of coffee and tea, but still new in the area of pepper.

And so I began to spread the word in the world of gastronomy, distributing samples to restaurateurs and chefs. In the morning, I sold pineapples, my favored fruit. In the afternoon, with Michelin Guide in hand, going page by page, 1, 2, 3, I spread the Penja pepper message among the chefs. Then across France, department by department, I preached the message to the finest épiceries. It was all a matter of persistence, patience and confidence!

Knowing that the main threat to pepper and spices in general is exposure to light, I worked with designer friends Florence and Patrick de Font-Réaulx to create an opaque and hermetically sealed pack that would give Penja pepper a protective screen. That was the starting point for a range that today covers more than four hundred items, and the packaging was, for two years, the feature that distinguished our range from others. Within the exotic fruit business as a whole, the sale of several bags of Penja pepper may have counted for little in the early years of Terre Exotique. But little by little a balance was established, until eventually I could choose to focus exclusively on spices, and pepper in particular.

Today, Terre Exotique is an adventure installed on the Loire with a team of some twenty people. Our main ambition is to place spice in its cultural, social and historical context... and to celebrate the marriage between civilization and gastronomy. That's why, for example, I do not try to create spice mixtures, because there's no good reason to re-invent what already exists. Don't forget that what's new for us is not new for the native people. The idea of discovery is entirely relative. We do not come as conquerors!

Therefore, what's most important is to study each spice in the place where it grows, to stay close to the area of production, to protect the freshness of the products, then try to get the most from them. Every day I am struck by the infinite and exceptional variety in pepper. It's a way forward, a route, with no fixed goal and no limit, given the extraordinary diversity at our disposal. The huge aromatic variety is an invitation to imagination and creativity, and all you need to express it is a simple grinding tool! To speak of pepper does of course require some knowledge. Would you ever confuse a tomato with a zucchini? Of course not! So to help make pepper more accessible, this book provides you with a system of classification. No, I don't expect to change the face of the world with pepper, berries and wild seed heads. But seed by seed, I do hope to play my part in the understanding of botanical diversity and the importance of preserving it...

Erwann de Kerros

Piper nigrum,
a bunch of fresh green pepper.

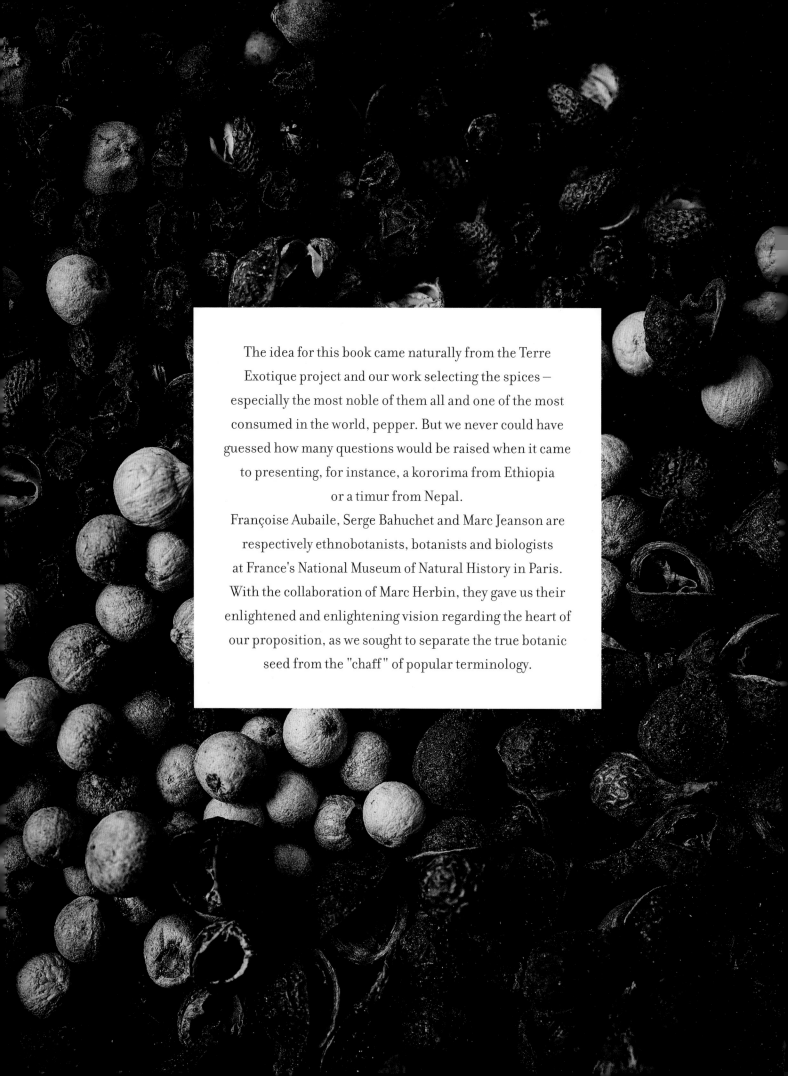

The idea for this book came naturally from the Terre Exotique project and our work selecting the spices — especially the most noble of them all and one of the most consumed in the world, pepper. But we never could have guessed how many questions would be raised when it came to presenting, for instance, a kororima from Ethiopia or a timur from Nepal.

Françoise Aubaile, Serge Bahuchet and Marc Jeanson are respectively ethnobotanists, botanists and biologists at France's National Museum of Natural History in Paris. With the collaboration of Marc Herbin, they gave us their enlightened and enlightening vision regarding the heart of our proposition, as we sought to separate the true botanic seed from the "chaff" of popular terminology.

Let's start with the general term "spices", which is so abused. If we work back through history, what are the main semantic – and therefore cultural – phases that we can identify?

Françoise Aubaile: The term 'spices' originally came from the Latin word 'species'. Up to the 17th century, it referred to everything sold by what the French would have called an *épicier*, which is to say dry goods brought from afar, shipped by Arab boats, then by traders from Venice, Genoa and Pisa. It could be rice or sugar, or a spice as one understands it in today's language. In our societies, their use was henceforth almost exclusively culinary. But it must be remembered that with their rich secondary components (essential oils, for instance) spices were first mainly recognized for their therapeutic powers (anti-bacterial, antispasmodic, etc.). In this context, they were used in Western medicine until the 19th century and are still used today in traditional treatments. To increase their efficacy, the societies of India, the Middle East and North Africa combined spices, and sometimes a great number, in groups recognized for their synergistic power. Examples are the garam masalas and Indian curries, the ras-el-hanout of North Africa, the colombo of the West Indies, and also France's aioli and pesto from Genoa.

From what period do we see spices used in the kitchen?

Serge Bahuchet: Looking back to ancient times, we can see several plausible archaeological indications of various plants being used to modify the taste of basic foods. We find phytoliths (crystals of vegetable cells) stuck to fragments of pottery, 6,000 years old in Denmark (garlic plant), 4,500 years old in India (ginger and turmeric) and 3,500 years old in various European countries (poppy seeds). This use of spices relates simply to the style of cuisine. Beyond that,

THE
TRUE SEED
AND ITS
IMITATORS

——————————

based on theories that are more or less proven, it seems that spices were notably used to conserve food, having an antifungal property, for instance.

F.A.: It is not entirely sound to think of spices used only for their antibacterial properties, since in largely vegetarian India spices were used as much with vegetables as with meat. The taste and the pleasure were equally important, if not more so. What's more, pepper has no antibacterial property in itself. That's why, in numerous preparations, it is always used with other things. In our Western cultures, to add pepper seeds to one's food was a mark of distinction! It was an exotic touch that signaled a higher social status and an openness to the world at large.

And within this large spice family, there is pepper. We call it the "king of spices" and it is surrounded by many connotations. But what do we actually mean by "pepper"?

S.B.: The word "pepper" comes from *pipalli*, from the Sanskrit word *pali* which refers to *Piper longum*. In the 4th century BC, the Greeks transformed the word *pipali* to *peperi*, from which came the Latin *piper*. From the 12th century, we see the form *peivre* and its derivatives, then in the following century the French word *poivre*.

F.A.: From an ethnobotanical point of view, we can say that from the 4th century BC, the words "pepper" or *poivre* were used to refer to whatever had a hot or piquant flavor. It was the analogous organoleptic character that gave rise to all these "*poivres de*" that are not actually part of the *Piper* family. In ancient texts, it's the taste that is the determining factor. In addition to the notion of usage. A pepper is something edible that has a particular application in cooking.

Erwann de Kerros: And if we concentrate on usage, then we can say that the pepper is a fruit*, which might be crushed, ground or powdered... for seasoning purposes.

Let's now consider the botanical dimension, which might just bring some order to all of this!

Marc Jeanson: In botanical terms, you have to wait until the 18th century and the Swedish naturalist Linnaeus before things get settled. With the Linnaeus classification, plants were no longer described by Latin polynomials, i.e. little phrases linking names to a number of adjectives. Henceforth the name was binomial. That is to say, one word for the genus qualified by a second word for the species within the genus. And so in botanical terms, the scientific name for pepper became *Piper nigrum*, *Piper longum*... belonging to the order of the Piperales and the family Piperaceae. The classification that Linnaeus established – with a hierarchy of kingdom, class, order, family, genus and species (as used in this book) – steadily became in the 19th century the standard nomenclature. The system is based on the reproductive system of a plant and makes no reference to its uses. When botanists are working with *Pipers*, they make no reference to the piquant taste. It's the physical description that interests them. All of the species of *Piper* that were subsequently discovered in the forests of America and Asia could be placed in the genus that Linnaeus had created. Botanically, for us, that's where it starts, and it helps us to find common factors, gives us a better understanding! Much later, taxonomists moved beyond the basic description of living organisms and sought to understand the family relationships between them (linked to the emergence of the theory of evolution). Evolutionary family trees could be constructed.

F.A.: That's true from a scientific point of view. But from a popular point of view, nothing has changed...

S.B.: The only true pepper is *Piper*, which falls plainly into a botanical category that corresponds to a certain genus or family (the Piperaceae, see p.33) but there are also terms that relate to usage and in part to commerce. It is the ethnobotanist's field only to define limits for the words used to denote vegetable species. For us in France, what we call in common language *poivre* "de"

something – *de Sichuan*, for example – does not correspond to a pepper in the strict botanical sense. This level of interpretation corresponds to commercial product names, which have added to the confusion. When someone refers to *poivre du Japon*, meaning the Sanshô berry, this is actually a *Zanthoxylum* of the Rutaceae family (and so not a Piperaceae), same as *poivre de Sichuan*. It's named partly by way of analogy and partly for purely commercial reasons, because these names – Japan, Sichuan – are more saleable. And there's a long list of such substitutes. In the course of the 15th century, as the use of spices became more common, they lost their market value and were overtaken by new varieties that were rarer and more expensive. For example in the 14th century, black pepper was replaced by the more fashionable Melegueta or grains of Paradise, *Aframomum melegueta* (Zingiberaceae). Long pepper then replaced the Melegueta in the 15th century. The American hot chili pepper, the Asian peppers in the 16th century, and so on. But the chili was an exception because it could be cultivated* and was therefore less expensive. Its success was also linked to the fact that at the end of the 15th century, the Spice Route was permanently shut off by the powerful Ottoman Empire, which established itself in the Middle East and controled the Indian Ocean routes up until the establishment of the Portuguese in the Far East, in the middle of the 16th century. The Portuguese themselves were then driven out in the course of the 16th century by the Dutch.

M.J.: It should also be remembered that at the time we didn't know much about "pepper". We needed a more exhaustive inventory of the tropical forests to give us a better understanding of the diversity of the *Piper* genus. For a very long time, even in the 18th century, we didn't yet have the global understanding of pepper that we have today. One spoke of spices in the general sense without understanding their full biodiversity*. This we only began to understand at the end of the 19th century and beginning of the 20th century.

Conservation is one of the subjects that occupy the researcher-teachers of the National Museum of Natural History in Paris. If we now look to the future, what is the position of the museum's researchers on measures to protect, conserve and recognize these spices, and most especially these different varieties of pepper?

S.B.: There are real risks of over-exploitation with wild plants that are harvested in nature, like the timur berry, if we increase the volume gathered and expand their market. If we want to meet the objectives of resource conservation and prevent over-exploitation, we should look at ways to rationalize gathering and introduce cultivation trials, so far as is possible without destroying the natural balance. The black pepper liana is one of the plants in these agro-forests that we can take as an example. The people of Indonesia have developed a form of managed forest with an interesting crop rotation model (see "Indonesia", p.124). First, the farmers fell a small area of forest and plant rice, leaving in place several "useful" trees (plants that bear fruit or produce resins, for instance). Then after harvest, they leave the forest to grow back, and they add to it by introducing useful plants (rattan, coffee and other fruit-bearing species). Pepper lianas then attach to the trunks of the trees... In this way, useful anthropic* forests develop across the decades. These are the agro-forests, which are now the model for the sustainable maintenance of tropical forests.

Close-up view of Batak berries ready to harvest,
Sumatra, Indonesia.

Françoise Aubaile
is an ethnologist with the CNRS within the eco-anthropological and ethnobiological team linked to the National Museum of Natural History in Paris. She specializes in the study of naturalist knowledge, the history of the spread of edible plants and scents in the Arab-Muslim world.

Serge Bahuchet
is an ethnoecologist and professor at the National Museum of Natural History in Paris. He specializes in the study of relationships between human societies and the natural environment. His principal theatres of research are Central Africa, Mexico and Guyana.

Marc Herbin
is a biologist, specializing in comparative anatomy. He is responsible for the conservation of the collections of anatomical samples in fluid at the National Museum of Natural History in Paris.

Marc Jeanson
is a botanist specializing in palms and responsible for the herbarium at the National Museum of Natural History in Paris.

Erwann de Kerros
is the founder of Kerex, a company that selects and distributes more than four hundred spice variants under the brand name Terre Exotique. An important part of the range is devoted to pepper.

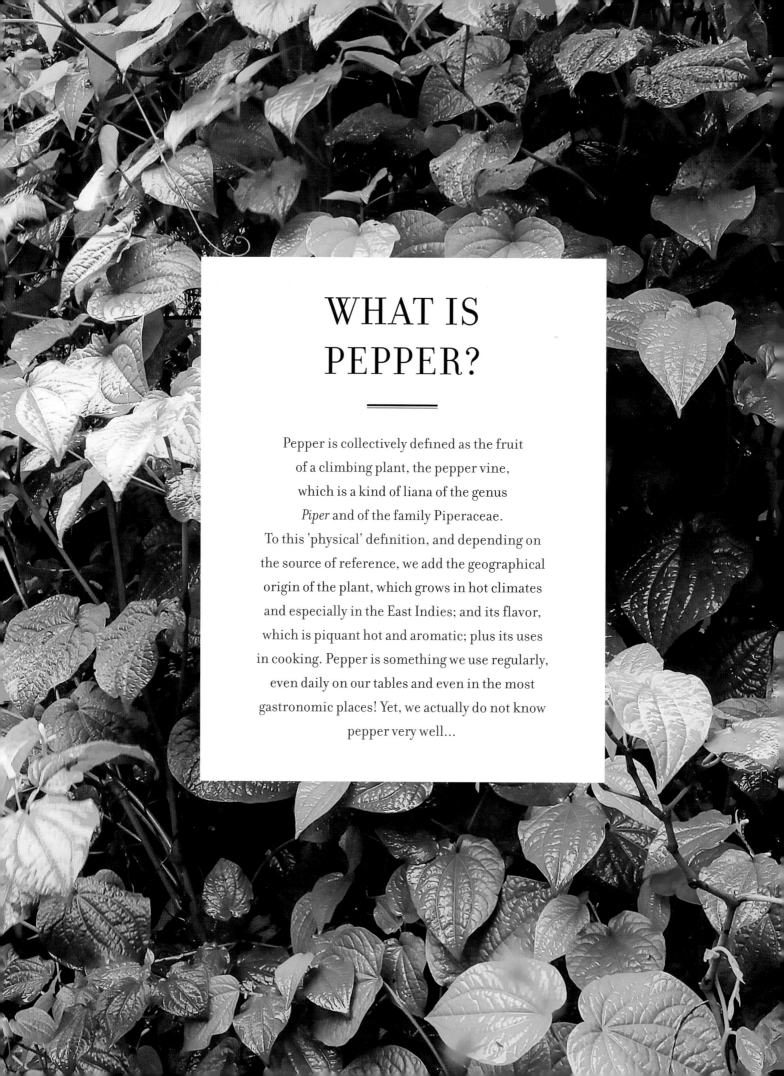

WHAT IS PEPPER?

———

Pepper is collectively defined as the fruit
of a climbing plant, the pepper vine,
which is a kind of liana of the genus
Piper and of the family Piperaceae.
To this 'physical' definition, and depending on
the source of reference, we add the geographical
origin of the plant, which grows in hot climates
and especially in the East Indies; and its flavor,
which is piquant hot and aromatic; plus its uses
in cooking. Pepper is something we use regularly,
even daily on our tables and even in the most
gastronomic places! Yet, we actually do not know
pepper very well...

Pipalli, Peperi, Piper...

The word "pepper" comes from *pipalli* (sometimes written *pippali*), from the Sanskrit *pali*, which towards the 4th century BC became *peperi*, then *piper* in Latin. The form *peivre* and its derivatives appeared in the 7th century, followed by the French word for pepper – *poivre* – in the following century. In his history of plants written in the 4th century BC, Theophrastus names India, Judea and Syria as the countries from which spices came. He speaks of two kinds of pepper reaching the Mediterranean. Theophrastus calls black pepper '"the Knidos berry", named after the town via which this spice arrived (located in present-day Turkey). The pepper that was the source of the name *Piper* was *Piper longum* and not *Piper nigrum* (which is the most common pepper); the ancient history of black pepper is often linked to and confused with the history of long pepper. The Romans used both variants (*longum* and *nigrum*) without distinction, and identified a third, white pepper, without realizing that this was actually black pepper with its cuticle removed (see "the colors of pepper", p.20).

A Rare and Costly Spice

While the Greeks and Romans knew the two spices (*longum* and *nigrum*) and recorded them, they were ignorant of their exact origins. Only the most affluent people used them, on special occasions. By the end of the classical age, pepper was known for its very substantial price. For example, it is said that in the year 410, in return for raising the third siege of Rome, the Goth Alaric demanded 5,000 pounds of gold, 30,000 pounds of silver, 4,000 robes of silk, 3,000 scarlet-dyed hides, precious furniture, ivory beds, tables in gold and silver and 3,000 pounds of pepper. And it was this 3,000 pounds of pepper that was the most difficult demand to fulfill, due to its rarity and cost, being imported from the Indies.

A Spicy Confusion!

The discovery of chili peppers (*Capsicum* spp.) in New Spain (Mexico) turned the world of spices on its head. Referred to as "native pepper" or "West Indian pepper", chilies came to Spain with the first voyage of Christopher Columbus, and were planted in Mediterranean gardens. The Spanish language is the root of this confusion, using the name *pimienta* for pepper (*Piper*) and *pimiento* for chili (*Capsicum*). In all the writings of the 18th century, the term "pepper" could refer to either plant, distinguished only by various adjectives.

Piment, the French word for chili, comes from the Latin *pigmentum* (meaning a colored material for painting, make-up or perfume), hence *pigmentarius* (a merchant of colors and perfumes). In the Middle Ages, it signified aromatic goods and spices, and later a spiced wine. In the same spirit, it is interesting to note the French word *poivrot* – a reminder that wines were once spiced (*poivré*)!

The Pepper
in our Kitchens

It must be remembered that according to the official classification established in the 18th century and brought to order by the Swedish naturalist Linnaeus, only the fruits of *Piper*, subdivided by species, *nigrum* (Penja, Kampot, Tellicherry pepper...), *longum* (Java pepper...), *cubeba* (Indonesian tailed pepper...), *borbonense* (the voatsiperifery from Madagascar...) have the right to use the term "pepper". From a botanical point of view, we still retain this definition, which reserves the denomination "pepper" for certain species of the genus *Piper* in the family of the Piperaceae. In the 18th century and the beginning of the following century, at the moment when we began to understand pepper better and describe their uses more precisely, the botanical concept and the ethnological perspective chose different definitions and reflected different realities. The ethnological perspective extended the notion of belonging to a certain botanical family to embrace the realities of usage and custom, both cultural and general, especially in a culinary context. For illustration, if you lived in China you would use Sichuan berries, sometimes called "Sichuan pepper", and if you lived in Cameroon, you would season your food with Penja pepper. The first comes from a dried seed head from a Chinese tree of the genus *Zanthoxylum* in the Rutaceae family, and the second, which is a pepper in the strict sense, comes from a liana of the *Piper* genus. In terms of usage, even though one is a pepper in botanical terms and the other is not, both are crushed or ground and used to give a more or less piquant flavor to your dish. That's why, based on a logic of analogy founded on their piquant flavor, termed "peppery", these types with different botanical characteristics and distinguished by a range of aromas have retained the popular name "pepper" and play their part in this collective group, without their being ranked in value from a taste point of view. If we accept the ethnobotanical view based on the common terms that we all use, then you'd say that pepper is just a whole spice that you can grind, crush, mill or infuse, used in cooking to give a more or less piquant taste in the mouth.

Let us set aside the distinction between "true" and "false" pepper, which has only gained ground in recent decades, based on a relatively recent botanical perspective (dating from the 18th century). What we have chosen to do here is present a selection of plants of different botanical families (Piperaceae, Rutaceae, Zingiberaceae...) that do all the same share similarities in terms of their usage and are all in our view of high quality. So feel free to enjoy the discovery of these "peppers", their history, the practices with which they are associated and above all, their extraordinary aromatic palette! Study them, smell them, taste them whole, crushed and infused, and experience them in tasty recipes that display their qualities to the fullest.

Black pepper is a fruit, a seed encased in a fleshy part, these two parts making up the fruit. White pepper is the seed from which Man has deliberately removed the fleshy part, known as the pericarp*, leaving the seed bare.

The Main
Producing Countries

Across the ages, *Piper nigrum* has established itself across the tropical belt of our planet. World production – taking black and white pepper together – was more than 450,000 tons in 2015, 10% more than in 2014 and 80% more than in 1995.

Today the main production areas are Vietnam (around 140,000 tons), India (around 85,000 tons), Indonesia (70,000 tons), Brazil (around 40,000 tons), China (around 85,000 tons), Sri Lanka (around 30,000 tons) and Malaysia (around 24,000 tons).

By way of comparison, the annual production of Penja pepper in Cameroon (see "Cameroon", p.40) is estimated to be 40 tons! An insignificant quantity compared to the giants of Asia. Asia accounts for 45% of world consumption, with India and China being the two countries that consume the most.

In 2015, Europe consumed around 90,000 tons, North America consumed 80,000 tons and the whole of Africa consumed "only" 25,000 tons, or 5.5% of the world total.

VIETNAM
140,000 TONS

INDIA
85,000 TONS

INDONESIA
70,000 TONS

BRAZIL
40,000 TONS

CHINA
38,000 TONS

SRI LANKA
30,000 TONS

MALAYSIA
24,000 TONS

CAMEROON
40 TONS

SOURCE: INTERNATIONAL PEPPER COMMUNITY

The Colors of Pepper

The best known type of pepper, *Piper nigrum*, from the Piperaceae family, can be green, black, white, red or grey, depending on its degree of ripeness at the point of harvest and the type of preparation and treatment.

Green pepper is harvested once the bunch has formed and the still-immature berries have grown to their adult size. It has to be conserved in a humid atmosphere. Green pepper is rarely sold in its fresh state and is most often offered freeze-dried, dehydrated or in brine. It is mainly used for the extraction of essential oils in the pharmaceutical, cosmetic and chemical industries. It had its moment of glory in French kitchens several decades ago thanks to certain emblematic recipes like Claude Terrail's stuffed duckling au poivre vert at the Paris restaurant La Tour D'Argent. The recipes in this book include some original ways to use green pepper (see p.206 and 222).

Black pepper comes from berries picked before complete maturity. The drying of the berries triggers a micro-fermentation inside each seed, and this gives the peppercorn its wrinkled appearance and a color between brown and black. The seeds are washed then sorted by hand to eliminate impurities. A hundred kilos of green pepper yields around thirty kilos of black pepper and some twenty kilos of white pepper.

White pepper is made with ripe berries stripped of their pericarp. As they ripen in the bunch, the berries turn an orange color, and it is at this point that they are picked. The seed that will become white pepper is soaked in spring water for eight to ten days, stirred every evening, and the water is changed every two days. The flesh softens and, at the end of ten days, the seed is washed again with a generous quantity of water. This operation is called retting. The seeds are then sorted and winnowed to remove the pericarp, leaving only the heart of the seed, which is left in the sun in a drying area for three to four days, depending on the strength of the sun. Once completely dry, the peppercorns are light colored, nearly white. While black pepper tends to dominate the market in general, Cameroon is one of the rare countries to exploit its white pepper and make it a specialty (see "Cameroon", p.40).

Red pepper is pepper that has fully matured in the bunch. This gives it a red color, close to the color of coffee beans. Red pepper is rarely consumed in this state and is mostly dried like black pepper. But it is soaked in hot water before drying to help it keep its color. Don't ever expect to see a cherry-red pepper! The berries are most often picked before maturity for economic reasons or reasons of climate, and they are rarely seen on the market.

Grey pepper is ground black peppercorns. It is the grinding of the black pericarp (the external flesh) together with the white inside that gives it the grey color — it owes its color to its usage. From an organoleptic and gastronomic point of view, we prefer pepper to be crushed or ground just before it is used.

Penja pepper, Cameroon.
It is time to harvest when one-third of the bunch is red.
White pepper is then made by removing the pericarp from the fruit.

Following two pages:
Batak berries at the point of maturity. Lake Toba, Sumatra, Indonesia..

TASTING

There are three steps to tasting pepper: observation; smell, or nosing the pepper in all its forms (whole, crushed, infused, etc); and taste, analyzing how the aromas develop in the mouth.

With practice, you will become more attuned to the specific characteristics of each family of pepper and the physical properties imparted by different methods of cultivation. You will also learn to define the flavor profile of whole peppercorns in all their richness and diversity…

But it would be quite wrong to think of tasting as a one-off experience consisting of a single sensory evaluation. Generally speaking, every tasting exercise requires the taster to explore their personal sensory memory bank. What goes for wine also goes for spices; there is more to tasting than following an analysis grid. Summoning up past experiences and emotions is quite as important as evaluating the appearance, nose and palate in more "technical" terms.

Within this highly complementary and all-encompassing vision of tasting, pepper and other spices, like wine, are seen as the product of a combination of natural and man-made factors – the coming together, with varying degrees of success, of the climate, the soil, the botanical variety and human skills. The influence of these factors is plainly revealed by the sensory evaluation of pepper from different production regions.

Tasting pepper and other spices takes time. Aroma development can sometimes be a very slow process. But your patience will be rewarded by the discovery of those subtle, complex notes, akin to those in great wine, that are released when freshly ground pepper is given time to breathe or to infuse. Pepper is a living product with highly volatile aromas. Sudden changes in temperature and oxygenation can have an overwhelming effect – a point well worth remembering in the heat of the action!

The tasting grid below has been specially designed to help you get the most out of the experience and raise your sensory awareness. Above all, remember that it is by learning to identify and recognize the aromas in pepper that you will discover all of their culinary possibilities…

The Aroma Families

To simplify the pepper tasting experience, the aromas characteristic of pepper have been classified into families, which are themselves further divided into subfamilies. Identifying these different aroma families is a lot of fun – conjuring up sensory memories, delving into your personal memory bank and building on it as you grow in experience. Some of the scents in pepper are easy to identify because they remind us of the smells we encounter every day (fruits, flowers, bread and milk, for example). Others are not so easily detected. We are all familiar with so-called "bad" smells like gasoline, burnt rubber or urine. But it takes practice to recognize the scent of Linden blossom, or the aromas of cherry pits or that touch of underbrush.

Aroma Families and their Signature Aromas

The taste characteristics of the peppers presented in this book may be classified into seven main families.

SPICE/BALSAMIC

Spice
licorice, vanilla, cinnamon, nutmeg, paprika, cloves, star anise, fennel, ginger, juniper, basil, spearmint, peppermint, thyme, rosemary, *garrigue* (Mediterranean scrubland), bay leaf, angelica, vanilla pod, garlic, onion...

Balsamic
resin, pine, sandalwood, beeswax, balsam, thuja, turpentine, camphor, cade oil...

PATISSERIE/DAIRY

Patisserie
honey, fresh bread, brioche, fruitcake, gingerbread...

Dairy
milk, cream, yoghurt, freshly churned butter, rancid butter...

ANIMAL

meat juices, leather, fur, game, civet (wild cat), musk, venison, civet (typically jugged hare or rabbit), stews, meat flavors, charcuterie, blood, animal skin, amber, fur, wet wool, male goat, musky, ripe meat, henhouse, tripe, stable, briny...

HERBACEOUS/VEGETAL

Herbaceous
herb condiments (fennel, anise, parsley, sage, coriander...), greenery (cut grass, box tree, ivy, budding blackcurrant, vine leaf, bay leaf, tobacco leaf...), *garrigue* (thyme, rosemary...), wild herbs (lemon balm, verbena, mint, eucalyptus...), dried herbs (straw, Virginia tobacco, Caporal tobacco, Havana cigars, tea, hay-making...)...

Vegetal
wood (dry wood, green wood, sawdust, oak, cedar, pine, sandalwood, rancio flavors in Cognac and Armagnac), underbrush (ferns, humus, wet earth, tree leaves, compost, lichen, dead leaves, moss...), fungi (fresh mushrooms, porcini, truffles...), green vegetables (asparagus, spinach, cress, cabbage, artichokes, French green beans...)...

FRUIT/FLORAL

Fruit
citrus (orange, grapefruit, lemon...), candied citrus (candied orange and lemon peel, candied orange and lemon, candied grapes...), red berries (raspberry, strawberry, redcurrants, gooseberry, wild strawberries...), black berries (cassis, black cherries...), wild berries (blackberries, blueberries, wild strawberries, cranberries...), fruits with pits (apricots, peaches, peach pits, mirabelle plums, bigarreau cherries, cherry pit, Kirsch...), fruits with seeds (quince, reinette apples, Golden Delicious, pears, fig, fresh grapes, muscat grapes, melon, fresh fig, medlars...), exotic fruit (bananas, pineapple, mango, litchi, passion fruit...), cooked fruit (stewed fruit, jam...), fruits in eau-de-vie (Morello cherries, plums...), dried fruit (dried apricots, bananas, figs and dates, prunes, raisins, nuts, hazelnuts, almonds, pistachios, bitter almonds...)

Floral
fresh flowers (white flowers, honeysuckle, linden flower, broom, jasmine, rose, iris, peony, violet, cherry, acacia, orange and peach blossom, hawthorn, dog-rose, geranium, magnolia, hyacinth, daffodil, citronella, heather, marshmallow (*Althaea officinalis*), carnation, gentian, chamomile, verbena, herb tea...), dried flowers (dried roses, chamomile, dried peony...)...

YEASTY/OXIDATIVE

Yeasty
green apples, bananas, hard candy, sour candy, acetone, yeast, leavened dough, soap...

Oxidative
candles, furniture polish, wheat, beer, cider, lees, lactic, milky, sour milk, sauerkraut, acetone...

CHEMICAL/EMPYREUMA

Chemical
medicinal, disinfectant, alcohol, cellulose, metallic, gasoline...

Empyreuma
chocolate, gingerbread, coffee, toast, caramel, smoke, soot, tar...

The Pepper-Tasting Technique

The technique used to taste pepper has a lot in common with the theory and practice of wine tasting. Interest in pepper-tasting as a way of learning more about pepper is relatively recent and attempts to rationalize the tasting process itself remain largely at the experimental stage. The emphasis is placed firmly on careful and meticulous evaluation, focusing on two areas of analysis: the creation of a specific aromatic profile for each different pepper family; and the definition of a sliding scale of strength, heat and intensity, modeled on the Scoville Scale.

APPEARANCE

The appearance of pepper (shape, color, size…) can tell you a lot about its plant family, including in some cases how it was grown. The little hole in a kororima pepper pod, for instance, tells you how the pepper was dried (strung on thread and hung up to dry, see "Ethiopia", p.146). Then there is the appearance of the pepper once it has been crushed – its color and texture may be indicative of its maturity.

NOSE

Smelling or "nosing" the pepper will tell you about its maturity and also how it was cultivated – the human factor, in other words. It will tell you whether the pepper was smoked, dried or perhaps lyophilized. Always take your time when nosing a pepper. Observe how the aromas reveal themselves and evolve over time. Ask yourself whether the nose is fruity, floral, woody, animal or spicy. Then draw on your sensory experience to describe how the pepper smells.

Nosing the pepper is the single most important part of the tasting. It is also the most complex and involves three separate phases.

The top notes (whole berries)

The "first nose" in wine parlance. Begin by smelling the pepper in its box, then in a small bowl to form an impression of its overall aromatic profile.

The middle or heart notes (crushed berries)

The "second nose" in wine parlance. Crush or grind the pepper seeds then smell them again, looking for more subtle aromatic nuances.

The base notes (crushed and infused berries)

The "third nose" in wine parlance. Leave the pepper to infuse in water heated to 158°F (70°C) then smell it again for a third and final time. Steeping brings out aromatic nuances, revealing the underlying complexity of the pepper's bouquet.

PALATE

There are three stages to assessing the palate, starting with the attack (the first impression that is formed as the taste buds come into contact with the pepper) and ending with the finish (discerning the pepper's aftertaste, its length on the palate and how it compares to the initial taste).

The attack

This is the first impression of the pepper in your mouth. Consider its moistness, fullness and fruitiness as you explore the taste from every angle.

Midpalate

This is the stage when you must attempt to oxygenate the pepper inside the mouth to assess its openness and acid structure. Known as retronasal olfaction, you exhale through the nose with the food in your mouth to increase the perceived intensity of the aromas. Notice the flavor, texture and structure of the pepper. It is the combination of the sensations experienced at this stage – smell, heat, touch – that will shape your overall impression of the pepper and its balance.

The finish

The third and final stage is to assess the length of the pepper's taste – its aftertaste or the persistence of its taste on the palate after you've swallowed.

TOUCH

Touching the pepper is appreciating how it feels in the mouth – its texture, essentially.

The *moelleux*

This translates to the perceived fatness, richness and smoothness of the pepper.

Acidity

Acidity is easy to identify since it is the acid content in the pepper that causes you to salivate. It is also what gives the pepper crispness on the palate.

Astringency

Astringency is the drying and sometimes puckering sensation produced by certain tannins.

Texture

This is essentially the "mouthfeel" or tactile sensation on the palate and is described using adjectives that borrow from various sources (textiles, geometry and anatomy, to mention but a few). There is the satiny feel of pink berries, the silky feel of Sanshô berries, the velvety feel of kororima berries and the soothing (sleep-inducing) feel of Sichuan berries…

BALANCE AND HARMONY

Balance

A pepper is said to be in balance when all of its tactile sensations (acidity, *moelleux*, astringency) are in equal proportion – neither too much nor too little.

Harmony

Harmony is the term applied to a pepper where everything comes together as an integrated whole – no harsh edges (bitterness), no jarring notes (tartness or sourness).

THE WORLD'S PEPPER

BY BOTANICAL FAMILY

Piperaceae
The Piperaceae

This family embraces some 2,750 species spread around the Tropics (Asia, Africa, America, the Pacific islands, etc.). Plants in this family may be bushes, lianas or herbaceous plants, of which some are epiphytes, meaning that their roots are not anchored in the soil like most plants, but attached to the branches or trunks of other plants that support them. One of the common morphological characteristics of all Piperaceae is the unique inflorescence comprising many small flowers on a dense spike (see illustration opposite).

The Piperaceae owe their name to the genus Piper, one of the most diverse members of this family, which includes among other things the various types of pepper. The term *piper* itself comes from *pipalli*, a word borrowed from the Tamil and Malayalam languages.

The Piperaceae are not heavily represented among northern flora, and were for a long time known only in Europe as berries sought and imported very expensively for their flavor. This phytochemical richness is displayed in a number of Piper species that have a range of uses. From classical times to the Middle Ages, various types of pepper were consumed (*Piper longum* L, *Piper cubeba* L, *Piper nigrum* L). The black pepper (*Piper nigrum* L) is the one most traded today, though In India and other Asian countries the long pepper and the cubeba are still much used, especially in ayurvedic medicine.

FAMILY
PIPERACEAE

GENUS
PIPER

SPECIES
NIGRUM

WHITE PENJA
PEPPER

ALSO KNOWN AS
BIRD'S PEPPER, MUNGO PEPPER

COUNTRY OF ORIGIN
CAMEROON

AN IMPLANTED* AND CULTIVATED SPECIES

Pepper was brought to Penja in Cameroon in the 1930s by Mr. Decré, a banana planter, and developed notably by Mr. Métomo and Mr. Aubriet. This is surely the most recent example of Piper nigrum planted outside its place of origin. Helped by the very favorable climatic conditions, the plantations have developed since that period to become in 2014 one of the first PGIs* on the African continent! Thanks to a volcanic terrain that is naturally rich and balanced, Penja pepper has outstanding character and taste.

In Cameroon, Piper nigrum is by tradition… white. The plantations of Penja have always produced white pepper, even though consumers and the trade in general favor the black. In Cameroon, demand is focused almost exclusively on the white pepper, which makes this an atypical case.

Cameroon is fortunate to have the precious natural spring water that is vital for the production of white pepper. But black pepper is easier to produce, so the price of Cameroon's white pepper is relatively high.

Today, Penja's small planters have grouped together for the development of the local culture and economy — initiatives that include social dimensions such as schools and working conditions…

APPEARANCE

Pretty round berries, uniform shape, quite smooth, predominantly creamy white in color but verging on light gray in some cases. White interior, with a rather matte, almost milky appearance.

NOSE

Top notes (from whole berries exposed to the air)
Menthol and vetiver stand out in a rather herbaceous nose, rapidly evolving toward enticing scents of fresh mint then hints of cold smoke. Wilder, more animal aromas follow a few minutes later.

Middle notes (from crushed and aerated berries)
The nose develops the piquancy of peppermint and burnt herbs — much like the smell of wet *garrigue* scrubland.

Base notes (from ground and infused berries)
Highly complex notes take shape, supported by a sweet, soft strength that hints at wilder aromas. Noticeable hints of musk and chicken stock plus a faint but enveloping smokiness rather like the smell of cold soot.

PALATE

Warm, spicy attack punctuated by sweet aromas of caramelized meat. Soft, musky notes intermixed with incense-like smells on the follow-through. Complex impression overall, triggering a slightly tingling oral sensation.
Good length, nice delicacy, with an herbaceous, animal-like character that confirms the dominance of animal notes on the nose. Powerful finish but smooth and sensual with enveloping, albeit subtle, tannins.

Aromatic families
Animal/Vegetal/Empyreuma

In cooking
A subtly delicious, intensely fragrant pepper that just begs for firm but delicately textured flesh — red meat, a fine cut of pork or free-range lamb. For best results, always grind the pepper just before serving to retain all of its freshness.

Recommended with
- sourdough toast drizzled with hazelnut oil;
- butter-roasted asparagus;
- oven-baked turbot basted with meat juices;
- smoked bacon wrapped chicken breast;
- braised fillet of beef or pork.

Recipe
Roasted turbot, kuri squash gnocchi, parsnip mousseline by Didier Edon, p.250

FAMILY
PIPERACEAE

GENUS
PIPER

SPECIES
NIGRUM

BLACK PENJA PEPPER

ALSO KNOWN AS
BIRD'S PEPPER, MUNGO PEPPER...

COUNTRY OF ORIGIN
CAMEROON

AN IMPLANTED AND CULTIVATED SPECIES

Penja pepper owes its outstanding character and taste to a volcanic terrain that is naturally rich and balanced. All stages in production (harvest, retting, drying, grading, sorting) are entirely manual, mainly in the expert hands of the village women. Penja pepper today enjoys a worldwide reputation.

Black Penja pepper is harvested before maturity, then dried in the sun in the province of Mungo. It is sorted peppercorn by peppercorn by the local women. White pepper may be Cameroon's flagship product, but for several years the Cameroonians have produced a small quantity of black pepper using a new technique: the pepper harvested in the morning is put in boiling water for several seconds, then immediately dried in the sun. This serves to stabilize the color of the peppercorns, while respecting hygiene standards.

NOSE

Dominant aromas of camphor and incense, evolving toward wild, pungent notes of musk and horse hide.

PALATE

Warm tangy, biting attack.
The finish leaves a heady, tannic impression reminiscent of the tannins in red wines.

Aromatic families
Balsamic/Fruit/Empyreuma

In cooking
For best results, always grind finely just before serving.

Recommended with
- summer vegetable *tian* (flan);
- pan-seared shrimp with Guérande salt;
- broiled lobster tail with brown butter;
- *rillettes* (potted meat) on a slice of brioche
- lacquered loin of free-range pork with sweet potato purée;
- honey-glazed pears.

Recipe
Cancale oysters in escabeche, coriander seeds by Olivier Arlot, p.212

FAMILY
PIPERACEAE

GENUS
PIPER

SPECIES
NIGRUM

GREEN PENJA
PEPPER IN BRINE

COUNTRY OF ORIGIN
CAMEROON

AN IMPLANTED AND CULTIVATED SPECIES

Green pepper is harvested before maturity when the seeds — some thirty per bunch — are still green. The seed is ripe for harvest if, when you squeeze it between thumb and index finger, it releases a whitish liquid. At this stage, the seed is not yet fully formed.

Green pepper is produced in all of the world's plantations. The difficulty is in conserving it. Left exposed to the air, the seeds turn black within several days. In Cameroon, the method of conservation is based on washing the bunches of green pepper in copious water, then pickling them in brine. The brine is prepared by filling a jar with water and adding an egg that settles at the bottom of the jar. Salt is then added until the egg floats to the top. The egg is removed, the green pepper is added and the jar is closed. Green pepper preserved like this can be kept for a year, stored away from the light — by which time, there will be a fresh harvest to replace it!

APPEARANCE

Long, bright green clusters, not unlike elderberry clusters, of perfectly round, uniformly shaped berries with a shiny appearance. The interior is fine-grained and firm with a milky white color.

NOSE

Top notes (from whole berries exposed to the air)
Floral, herbaceous nose of freshly mown grass, rapidly evolving towards a watermelon and fresh flower bouquet with just a whiff of aniseed. Wilder, garlicky aromas (chives) follow a few minutes later.

Middle notes (from crushed and aerated berries)
Piquant, more mentholated notes gradually emerge, with fairly powerful background aromas confirming the opening aromas of green garlic.

Base notes (from ground and infused berries)
With infusion, the vegetal-herbaceous nose unfolds one step at a time and oh so delicately, framed by underlying scents of cold smoke and soot that bring to mind the inside of damp cellars dug into tuffeau rock.

PALATE

Powerful attack, savory and piquant, punctuated by vegetal notes of crushed blackcurrant leaves. Crisp taste, good length, creating a tannic, burning sensation on the palate with accents of menthol. Softer notes of faded wild flowers appear a few seconds later.
Nice aromatic persistence and delicacy, with a rather vegetal profile recalling the skin of a granny smith apple. For all of its strength and piquant finish, this is quite a smooth pepper with no trace of aggressiveness. Ends with a harmonious chorus of flavors dominated by crystallized rhubarb and chives.

Aromatic families
Empyreuma/Vegetal/Floral

In cooking
A piquant, herbaceous pepper just made to go with strong textures and smoky flavors – grilled red meat for instance – but with a delicate, crisp, almost biting taste that will also complement creamy dishes (hot or cold). Infused into cream, it will really show its sweetness. To keep its bitterness at bay, we advise rinsing this pepper in cold water before grinding in a mortar.

Recommended with
- vegetable gratin;
- fresh river fish fry with tartar sauce and fresh tarragon;
- pan-fried shrimp with green garlic;
- pan-fried beef tenderloin, served with a Mediterranean vegetable *tian*;
- rump of veal with mousseron mushrooms (small wild mushrooms);
- broiled duck breast.

Recipes
Mackerel fillets and rillettes on toast by Didier Edon, p.206
Smoked salmon, celery, celery water by Olivier Arlot, p.222

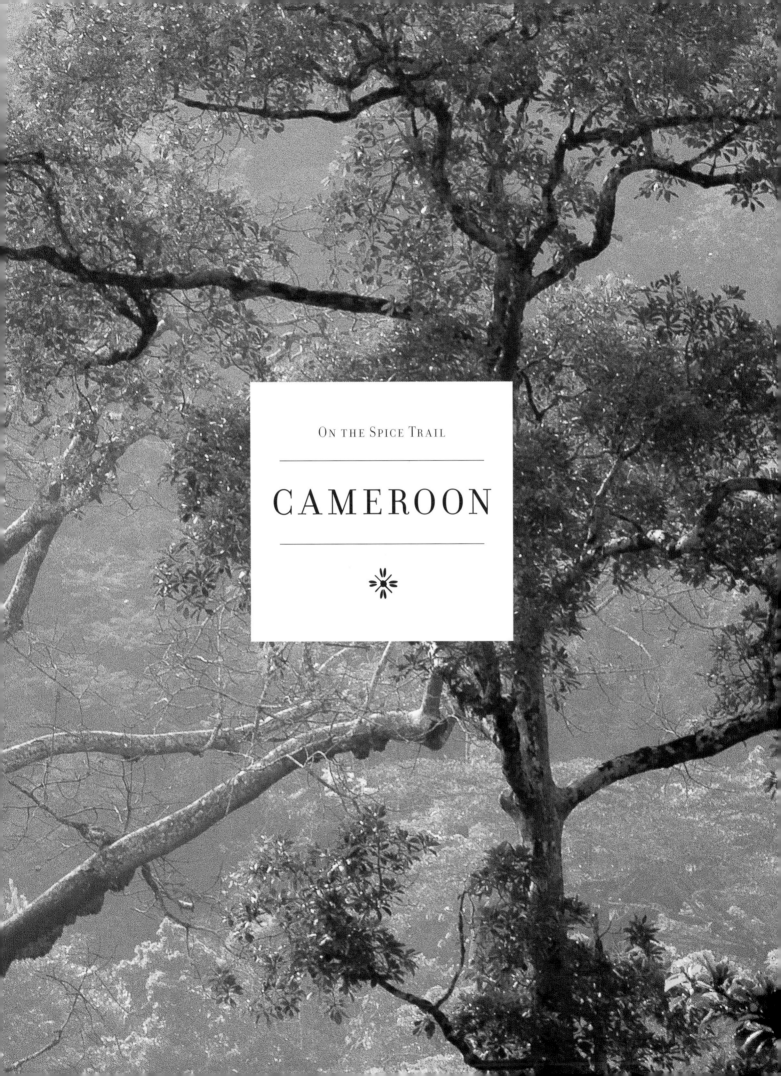

ON THE SPICE TRAIL

CAMEROON

Penja Pepper
The *Piper* I Love Most

It was 1992 when I was first drawn to the pepper vines, the way others have been drawn to the forests. Since then, Cameroon, and most especially Penja, have always been close to my heart. A trip there every two years, whether on the spur of the moment or planned, has kept me in touch with the Penja pepper vines, rather as one enquires after the health of an old friend...

I land in Douala, the business capital of Cameroon and center of the coastal region. This is my point of departure for Penja, less than two hours distant. I know this airport well, from the time when it carried me to my first encounter with pepper cultivation at the beginning of the 1990s.

I was 22 years old, with a brand new business school degree. I had several travel adventures under my belt, two teenage years spent with my family in N'Djamena in Chad, and my father had given me a taste for Africa...

This was my first serious job, my first engagement with agriculture, and my first encounter with Penja pepper. My first child...

These memories travel with me each time I journey to Cameroon, back to the Aubriet plantation where I took my first steps as a pepper planter. I remember the 5:30 am wake-up call, the wages, bi-weekly, the recruitment of pickers for the harvest... At the entrance, I see that white cross that the workers say provides protection, for the place itself and for the men and women who work there.

Such are the emotions evoked by the spirit of the plantation, a spirit that seems fixed in the colonial age. Each time I return, the memories return too, as I take stock of changing realities in a country that finds itself in a continuous state of evolution. Remember that it is only a few years since pepper in Cameroon was a very minor crop with little recognition. Penja is a place where you can grow anything! The fertile volcanic terrain and humid equatorial climate make this an ideal place for crops like pineapples, bananas, papaya, mango, avocado, cocoa and coffee – all supremely profitable and well established here for many years. Add to that a very strong agriculturally based social structure where everyone cultivates their own precious plot. The relationship between the people and the land is fundamental.

A track on the outskirts of the town of Penja leads to the pepper plantations that produce this local treasure. On this occasion, my visit has a surprising start as I find the Aubriet plantation altogether laid to waste, ravaged by *Phytophthora*, a major scourge in Cameroon that has destroyed two thirds of the plants. No sign of a crop. Virtually no vines. No one in charge – the plantation is abandoned. A sad conclusion. But on new plots in this same area, a hundred new pepper plantations of all sizes are now prospering and well organized.

That's the effect you get with a PGI*!

In 2013, Penja white pepper was among the very first agricultural products to be granted Africa's Protected Geographical Indication (PGI*). This three-letter distinction not only raises the status of pepper cultivation but also supports social projects that were quite simply unimaginable in earlier times. The most visible symbol of this wind of change in Penja is a new bilingual school for three hundred pupils – one of the initiatives led by Mr. René Claude Metomo and his wife.

The Harvest

In Cameroon, the harvest generally starts in February and continues for around two months. Several years ago, it would start in November-December. It is in any case vital that it is completed before the rainy season, which begins in Cameroon in April. Working from a bamboo ladder put together on the spot, the bunches are picked by hand, starting green at the beginning of the harvest then bit by bit turning red as maturity progresses. The harvesters visit each plant several times (three to five visits per plant). In ideal conditions, a good harvester can pick thirty to forty kilos of fresh pepper in a day.

Inside the green seed, the whitish liquid hardens and forms a white center, while the outer pericarp turns red. The riper the pepper, the redder it gets.

It is important to harvest the bunch when it is at least one third ripe, or even as much as half red. If you wait too long, the bunches will fall to the ground and the birds, who are very fond of pepper, will eat them.

The birds choose the berries that are the best looking and most ripe. When the bird expels this seed after eating, it will grow to form a particularly vigorous liana on the spot where it falls. Hence "bird's pepper", the original commercial name for Penja pepper!

A diversified, optimal growing technique for greater profitability?

There's been an evolution in the way pepper is cultivated in Penja. In the first year that new plots are worked, the producers plant papayas that have a lifespan of two to three years. Lianas are meanwhile planted between the rows of papayas, with poles to support them as they grow. The papayas serve to shade the pepper plants and are then cut down at the end of their productive life. This growing technique makes it possible to regulate sun exposure before the support poles are established, and also to stagger yields. It is four or five years before a pepper liana is productive, which represents a considerable investment period for local producers. Accepting a long-term investment without some immediate return is not an attractive proposition. This new and effective technique allows planters to accommodate the investment entailed in the planting of new pepper plots.

It was while visiting this Cameroon pepper plantation that I got to see the extraordinary labor entailed, most especially in sorting and processing which must be conducted in a manner that respects the hygiene regulations set by the PGI*. I talked with the pepper growers who now work as a group, discussing techniques, equipment, new developments and perspectives. We had interesting discussions about the degree of maturity of the pepper at the point of harvest, looking to obtain peppercorns that are fatter and better formed in order to raise quality. Tests are conducted on the spot, and they offer to send me samples... a collaboration is established and the discussion is very relaxed. My personal experience makes this easier: the four years I spent working on the Aubriet plantation, coupled with my efforts across the past two decades to raise the profile of white Penja pepper, here and elsewhere. This helped me to understand local issues and the constraints of the terrain. I found that the socio-economic results were very positive and the dynamic was very strong; many "small planters" were investing and working hard with the education of their children in mind! Penja is looking forward to its future with a smile. On the flipside of this coin, there were many local complaints about the inflation of the price of pepper. "Penja pepper has become too expensive," protests Maria Penja who is reputed to make "the best chicken in the area". Marie Penja and her roadside restaurant have been an institution for some thirty years, and she has needed no prompting from award-winning French chefs to use local pepper in the seasoning of her *poulet DG* ('DG' for 'Director General', to signify the status of this dish).

"Penja pepper has become too expensive!"

It was with Marie Penja that I went to the Wednesday market in Loum, where we found her friends along with a good number of spices, some endemic*, some wild*, as used by all the Cameroonian cooks: African nutmeg (ihiru/pebe), womi, malam berry, ganshu berry... So many names that differ from region to region, as I try with varying success to place them in botanical families! Malam would be a *Zanthoxylum*? Pebe, a *Monodora myristica*? And on these carpets of spices laid out before me, I see one of those treasures that in a split second justifies a journey across the world! A jujube, I am told. What I see is exactly like the kororima that thrilled me in Ethiopia (see p146). A Zingiberaceae? An *Aframomum*? Just to complicate matters further, this "jujube" is no relation of the jujube fruit.

Retting

The seed for making white pepper is set to soak straight away for eight to ten days in a large basin filled with spring water. It is stirred every evening, and the water, which turns brackish, is changed every two days. The flesh decomposes and at the end of ten days the seed is washed in a liberal quantity of water. That's when the heart of the pepper appears: the white pepper. It is then set to dry in a drying area for three to four days, depending on sunshine.

Grading and Sorting

The small peppercorns and the large peppercorns are now separated. The Cameroonian market prefers small peppercorns; the Western market prefers the large. From an organoleptic point of view, it is impossible to say whether the large peppercorn is better than the small.

The peppercorns are sorted one by one on a stainless steel table. At this stage, every last trace of waste is removed to make the pepper as homogeneous as possible. Daily output is around twenty-five kilos per sorter. All of these preparatory steps are carried out on the plantation.

Total production is only forty tons per year, which is insignificant on a world scale.

Used in Cameroonian cooking, it serves a symbolic function that is part of traditional culture, especially the coronation ceremonies of the Bamileke chiefdoms. The Bamileke come from the west of Cameroon and it has always been a sign of friendship among them to exchange these "seeds of peace" – you often spot them in the pockets of their shirts. They grow in the same conditions as the kororima – roots in water all year round. Their favorite spot is the permanent cloud of humidity at the base of the Ekom Nkam falls (as featured in the film "Greystoke: The Legend of Tarzan, Lord of the Apes").

I came here to Cameroon to take stock of Penja pepper. But as it turns out, several hours' walking brings me to a market where I discover other spices to identify and maybe a future seed to mill for Terre Exotique.

Sixteen years after my first Cameroonian adventure, it gives me special pleasure to see the positive initiatives supported by a band of committed producers. What's needed in this dynamic context is a balanced and lasting partnership within which producers and distributors can pursue their respective interests. Pepper cultivation is now thriving both locally and internationally, and has grown to become a profitable and significant element of agriculture. The Cameroonian example has inspired imitators and many African countries in the region are now eager to produce their own

pepper. What a pleasure it is to hear the men and women of the villages telling me that their pepper is quite simply "the best in the world"!

Malam

In the marketplace in Loum, among a great variety of Cameroonian spices, we discover the foliated berries of malam, a pepper previously unknown to us that serves as the basis for sauces in local cuisine (see p198).

47

FAMILY
PIPERACEAE

GENUS
PIPER

SPECIES
NIGRUM

BLACK KAMPOT PEPPER

COUNTRY OF ORIGIN
CAMBODIA

—

AN IMPLANTED AND CULTIVATED SPECIES

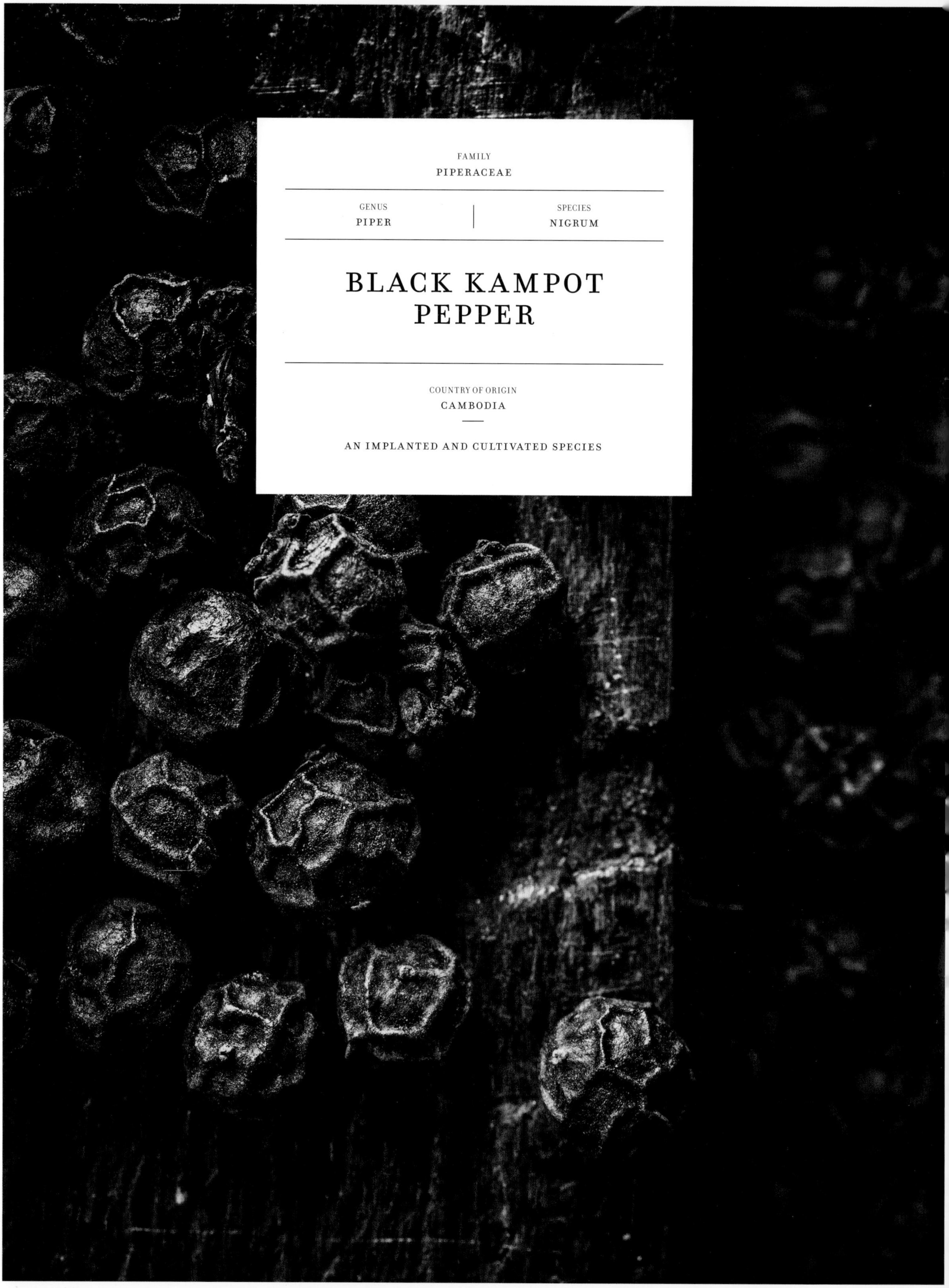

The history of Kampot pepper is tied in with the history of Cambodia: the waves of Chinese immigrants, the French protectorate, the civil war and the signs of a new economic revival in the country. We find evidence of this pepper in the kingdom of Angkor and most especially in the accounts of the travels of the Chinese explorer Zhou Daguan in the 13th and 14th centuries. Chinese immigrants from Hainan Island in the south of China were the ones who introduced the pepper to Kampot. They were already cultivating the pepper in China, but it was during the colonial period that Kampot pepper reached its apogee and became an import commodity of the first rank. From 1975, the Khmer Rouge cut production to nothing to make way for rice, and it is only thirty years later that several families of planters have given this pepper a new start. Situated between sea and mountains, these exceptional lands are today cultivated by families of planters who are devoted to their pepper and proud of their ancestral savoir-faire.

In 2009, Kampot pepper was the first Cambodian product to win Protected Geographical Indication (PGI*) status, thanks in particular to the support of a group of French producers who specialize in piment d'Espelette. Having a PGI increased the producers' revenue tenfold, proving the effectiveness of collaboration between producers at an international level. In February 2016, Kampot pepper won European recognition as an Appellation d'Origine Protégée (AOP), which not only served to discourage counterfeiting but also assisted well-priced exportation, especially to the European Union, the United States and Japan.

Black Kampot pepper is harvested and sorted by hand, then dried in the sun. It comes from the province of Kampot and from Kep in Cambodia.

NOSE

Fruit and menthol on the nose, delivering complex scents of green apples and pears with a subtle underlying hint of eucalyptus.

PALATE

Moderately piquant, with distinctive notes of camphor and peppermint.

Aromatic families
Fruit/Balsamic/Empyreuma

In cooking
Accents of fruit and menthol make this pepper the ideal ingredient for sweet and sour dishes. Grind using a pestle and mortal just before serving –prolonged cooking will accentuate its bitterness and is best avoided.

Recommended with
· pan-fried pike fillet with fresh broad beans;
· milk-fed veal roast with *mousserons*;
· roast guinea fowl with braised Chinese leaves;
· pan-fried candied cherries with green Chartreuse;
· fresh mint sorbet.

FAMILY
PIPERACEAE

GENUS
PIPER

SPECIES
NIGRUM

RED KAMPOT PEPPER

COUNTRY OF ORIGIN
CAMBODIA
—

AN IMPLANTED AND CULTIVATED SPECIES

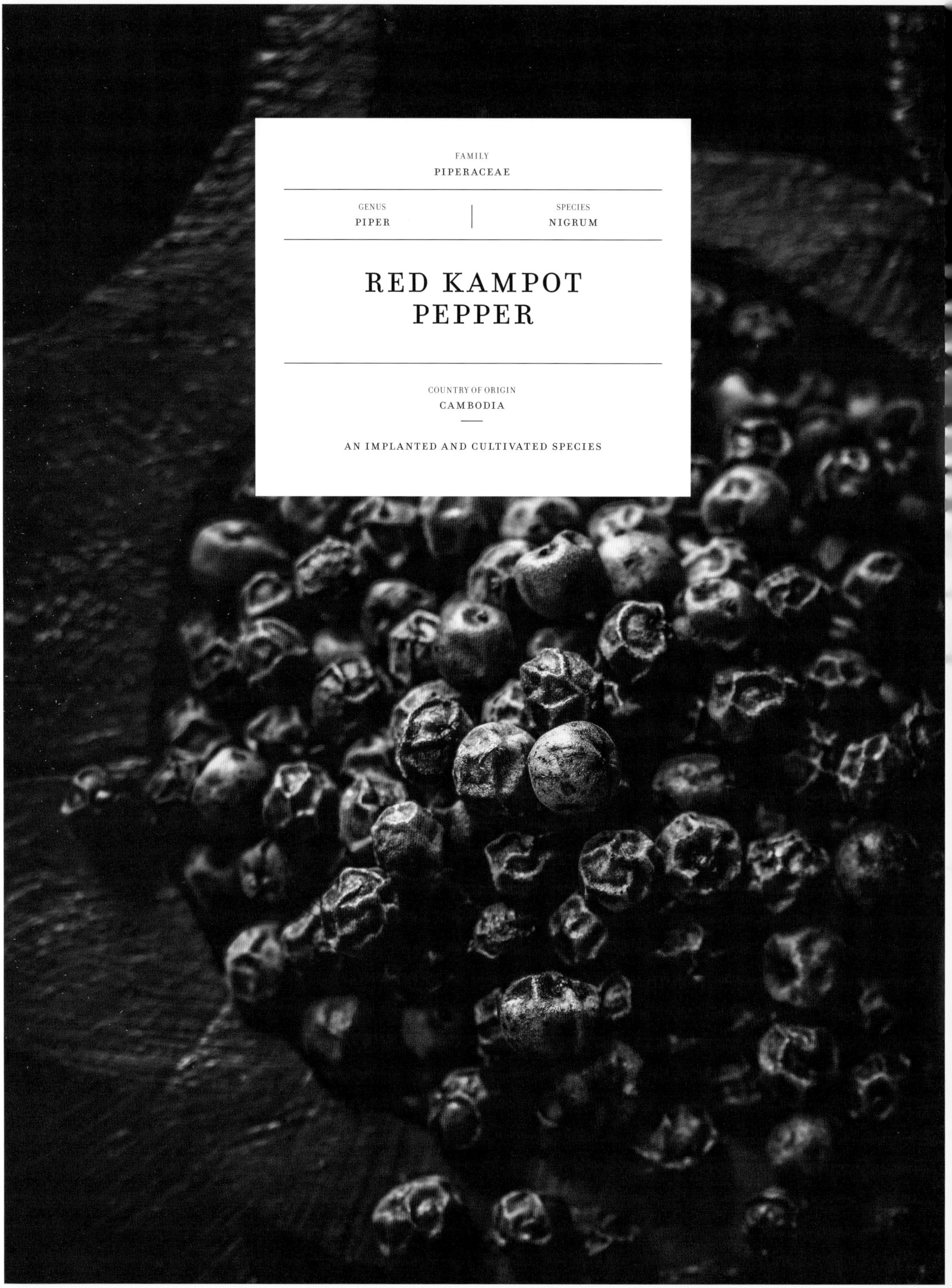

The history of Kampot pepper is tied in with the history of Cambodia: its waves of Chinese immigrants, the French protectorate, the civil war and the signs of a new economic revival in the country.

In 2009, it was granted PGI* status, and AOP status in 2016 (see black Kampot pepper on the previous pages).

Red Kampot pepper berries are harvested at full maturity. To preserve their full color, they are soaked immediately after picking in boiling water, then again in chilled water.

APPEARANCE

Pretty, medium-sized berries, perfectly round in shape with a dark garnet-red color, verging on brick red in some cases and quite shiny.
Slightly wrinkled pericarp with a jade green interior.

NOSE

Top notes (from whole berries exposed to the air)
A fruity, floral suggestion of red berry jam, followed by successive hints of morello cherries and small acidulous cherries that rapidly give way to more floral notes.

Middle notes (from crushed and aerated berries)
Leaving the pepper to breathe for a few minutes intensifies the nose, revealing crystallized fruit aromas of candied orange and lime peel plus more exotic scents such as lemongrass intermingled with touches of Bourbon vanilla.

Base notes (from ground and infused berries)
Infusing the pepper brings out the subtlety of the nose, which offers warmer, smoother scents of toast and toasted brioche with just a sprinkling of smoky, almost burnt notes.
Piquant smells of crystallized citrus then emerge, with hints of sweetness and softness that recall the delicate tang of orange candy.
The overall impression is one of great charm and intensity – a fragrance not unlike the aromas of jam and cherry liqueur (kirsch).

PALATE

Moderately piquant but very intense attack, with a slightly tangy taste that confirms the cherry notes on the nose, all wrapped up in green scents of citrus (lime and grapefruit).
That tangy, slightly sour taste becomes more pronounced, revealing an almost tannic framework infused with scents of lemongrass and dried flowers. Subtle persistence on the palate, plenty of length and intensity, with an impression of sweetness despite a piquant edge.
Charming, finesse-driven finish, the strength and piquant warmth of tart cherries combining with the delicate warmth of sweet, candied citrus enveloped in vanilla.

Aromatic families
Fruit/Balsamic/Empyreuma

In cooking
Notes of citrus and cherry invite pairings with sweet-and-sour dishes and foods with a slightly tart flavor (citrus) and a smooth, creamy texture (white poultry meat). For best results, grind the pepper coarsely just before serving to preserve its aromatic qualities.

Recommended with
- braised fillet of sea bass with citrus and lemongrass;
- free-range poultry;
- Géline de Touraine chicken cooked in a tajine;
- foie gras with a citrus reduction;
- baked loin of veal;
- soft goat cheese such as Sainte-Maure;
- pears and pink grapefruit turnover.

Recipe
Fillet of roe deer, salsify root and quince by Olivier Arlot p.266

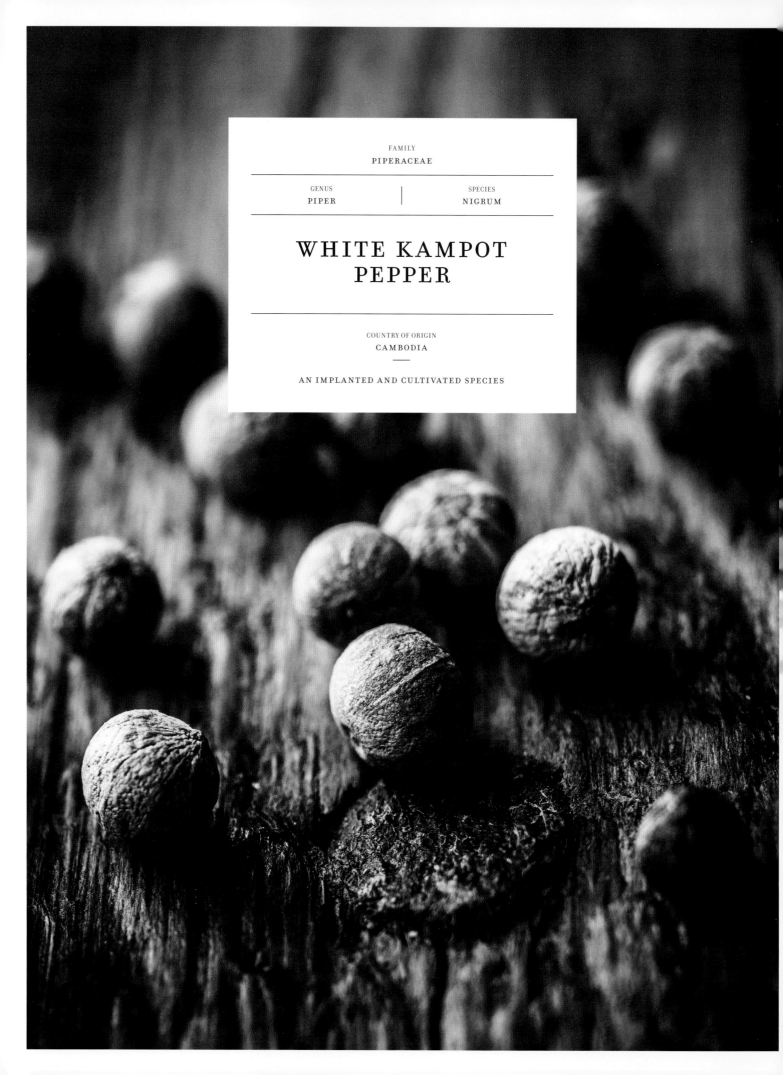

FAMILY
PIPERACEAE

GENUS
PIPER

SPECIES
NIGRUM

WHITE KAMPOT PEPPER

COUNTRY OF ORIGIN
CAMBODIA
—

AN IMPLANTED AND CULTIVATED SPECIES

Between sea and mountains, families of planters who are devoted to their pepper and proud of their ancestral savoir-faire cultivate the exceptional lands of Cambodia's Kampot and Kep provinces.

In 2009, Kampot pepper was the first Cambodian product to win Protected Geographical Indication (PGI*) status, which increased the producers' revenue tenfold, and proved the effectiveness of collaboration between producers at an international level. In February 2016, Kampot pepper won European recognition as an Appellation d'Origine Protégée (AOP), which not only served to discourage counterfeiting but also assisted well-priced exportation, especially to the European Union, the United States and Japan.

White Kampot pepper is harvested at full maturity. Every stage in its production (harvesting, retting, washing, drying, sorting) is done entirely by hand. After soaking in spring water for several days, the berries are stripped of their pericarp and dried in the sun.

NOSE

Top notes (from whole berries exposed to the air)
Intense notes of crystallized lemon and freshly-squeezed citrus juice on a vegetal nose with hints of dried grass, evolving a few minutes later towards notes of fresh mint.

Middle notes (from crushed and aerated berries)
Subtle fragrances of mint tea intermingled with hints of anise-infused concoctions conjure up images of a Mediterranean garden.

Base notes (from ground and infused berries)
Infusing the peppercorns releases a complex array of aromas – a blend of power with softness evolving toward sugary notes of cream and melted butter. Concentrating the aromas releases a whiff of aniseed-flavored patisserie.
These sweet flavors are then overtaken by sharper notes of orange.

PALATE

Warm, sensual attack, with prominent notes of sweet, fruity citrus juice. Good length, complex and intriguing with an impression of softness overlaid by a subtle piquancy.
These sweet flavors are then overtaken by sharper notes of orange and grapefruit swathed in camphor.
Plenty of length, delicate but somewhat vegetal and herbaceous on the palate, confirming the impression on the nose.
The finish retains a sweet, subtle touch of piquancy that adds special character.

Aromatic families
Fruit/Vegetal/Dairy

In cooking
A sweet, fragrant pepper partners perfectly with strong-flavored dishes. The perfect match for juicy white meat, such as a plump, roasted free-range chicken.

Recommended with
- smoked bacon and winter vegetable soup;
- géline de Touraine chicken poached in vegetable-citrus broth;
- soft-boiled egg with green asparagus;
- cod steak seared in olive oil;
- vegetable puree;
- mint tea.

Recipe
Pressed veal sweetbreads, salmon, artichoke by Didier Edon, p.208.

FAMILY
PIPERACEAE

GENUS
PIPER

SPECIES
NIGRUM

TELLICHERRY PEPPER

ALSO KNOWN AS
KERALA PEPPER, THALASSERY PEPPER...

COUNTRY OF ORIGIN
INDIA
—

A WILD AND CULTIVATED SPECIES

This pepper is native[*] *to Thalassery*, also known as Tellicherry, a town in the state of Kerala on the Malabar coast (known as the "spice coast") in southern India. The exceptional soils of this conspicuously humid region produce 70% of India's spice production. In 1708, the English built a fort here to control the region's trade in spices, including the celebrated and greatly coveted Piper nigrum. Originally no more than commercial in purpose, the English presence in India was to become the basis of a colonial empire.

APPEARANCE

Pretty, largish berries, round, uniform in shape, dark brown to black in color except for a few paler but more brilliantly colored, almost orange berries. Slightly wrinkled pericarp.

NOSE

Top notes (from whole berries exposed to the air)
An immediate departure toward warm yet fresh exotic notes – rare, tropical rainforest trees come to mind – following through with more floral aromas overlaying subtle hints of citrus.

Middle notes (from crushed and aerated berries)
Balsamic notes of cedar bark and fern to the fore, persisting against a backdrop of menthol and camphor aromas.

Base notes (from ground and infused berries)
The nose shows warmer notes of candied citrus peel, complemented by a smooth, faint sweetness suggesting the subtle flavor of tangy orange candy.

PALATE

Piquant flavors on attack tempered by a slight touch of sweetness, following through with intense notes of lemongrass and kumquat. The overall sensation is one of citrus-dominated crispness (freshly-squeezed grapefruit and lemon juice). Good aromatic persistence, quite piquant, with a tannic impression dominated by a slight bitterness (citrus). Warmth and a slight heat persist on the finish, gradually giving way to a crisp aftertaste showing notes of orange peel.

Aromatic families
Floral/Fruit/Herbaceous

In cooking
For lovers of piquant cuisine this exciting pepper offers real food for thought. Its notes of citrus and precious wood will bring out the delicate flavor of poached white fish as never before, to say nothing of its affinity for red meat (grilled or braised). For best results, grind using a pestle and mortar just before serving.

Recommended with
· rib of Parthenaise beef;
· veal sweetbreads in puff pastry;
· free-range poultry poached in a pig's bladder;
· roast pike perch steak with thyme;
· goat cheese;
· strawberry turnover with aged balsamic vinegar.

Recipe
Passionately passion fruit, white chocolate by Olivier Arlot, p.282

First planted in Vietnam by the French in the 17th century, this pepper was until the end of the 19th century mainly cultivated in Phú Quôc, Hòn Chông and Hà Tiên. It was at the beginning of the following century that it appeared in the southeast of Nam Bô, where most of the country's pepper cultivation is now concentrated.

The white pepper is made with ripe berries that have their outer layer (pericarp) removed (see "The colors of pepper", p.20). Harvesting is done manually, seed by seed. Then the pepper is dried in the sun for several days.

NOSE

Notes of caramelized spice stand out on a smoky, herby nose, evoking roasted chanterelle mushrooms with just the faintest vegetal suggestion of green tobacco, all underpinned by a menthol-like whiff of medicinal salve.

PALATE

Frank attack with good bite, showing intense flavors of roasted caramel and peppermint.

Aromatic families
Spice/Vegetal/Chemical

In cooking
For best results, avoid overheating this pepper otherwise it will taste bitter. Grind coarsely using a pestle and mortar.

Recommended with
· girolle and chanterelle mushroom sauté;
· roasted line-caught turbot basted with meat juice;
· a dark chocolate fondant with a fresh mint coulis.

FAMILY
PIPERACEAE

GENUS	SPECIES
PIPER	NIGRUM

BLACK NAM BÔ PEPPER

COUNTRY OF ORIGIN
VIETNAM
—

AN IMPLANTED AND CULTIVATED SPECIES

First planted in Vietnam by the French in the 17th century, this pepper was until the end of the 19th century mainly cultivated in Phú Quôc, Hòn Chông and Hà Tiên. It was the beginning of the following century that it appeared in the southeast of Nam Bô, where most of the country's pepper cultivation is now concentrated.

Vietnam is the world's leading exporter of pepper, with more than 90% of production going to export markets. Harvesting is performed manually, seed by seed. The black pepper comes from berries picked before complete maturity. It is the drying that gives the peppercorns their wrinkled appearance and color.

NOSE

Dominated by delicate aromas of ripe white fruit, showing real finesse as it evolves toward charming notes of roasted cocoa, dried flowers and exotic wood smoke.

PALATE

Hot, with good bite on the attack and woody flavors, all wrapped up in a surprising combination of sandalwood and balsam with an undercurrent of camphor.

Aromatic families
Fruit/floral/balsamic

In cooking
For best results, avoid overheating this pepper to keep its subtly fruity aromatics intact. Grind coarsely using a pestle and mortar just before serving.

Recommended with
- a port wine aspic;
- semi-cooked duck foie gras;
- roasted line-caught sea bass basted with meat juice;
- bittersweet chocolate crunch cake.

FAMILY
PIPERACEAE

GENUS
PIPER

SPECIES
NIGRUM

BLACK LAMPONG PEPPER

COUNTRY OF ORIGIN
INDIA

———

AN IMPLANTED AND CULTIVATED SPECIES

It was more than ten centuries ago when Indian traders introduced the first pepper plants throughout the Indian ocean, most especially in Indonesia, Java and Sumatra. Black Lampong pepper is grown in the far south of the island of Sumatra in Indonesia. It is harvested and sorted by hand in the province of Lampong, with the Java Sea on one side and the Indian Ocean on the other. Lampong mainly produces black pepper, which is easier to produce than white pepper that requires copious water and extra equipment such as soaking basins (see "Indonesia", p.132).

NOSE

Slightly nutty on the nose, notes of dried fruit intermingled with camphor-like fragrances, evolving towards smoky, sooty scents.

PALATE

Frank attack, plenty of heat and bite, finishing on an impression of menthol freshness with a marked smoky, exotic wood edge.

Aromatic families
Fruit/Balsamic/Empyreuma

In cooking
For best results, grind coarsely using a pestle and mortar just before serving.

Recommended with
· salt-crusted sea bream with potatoes;
· whole salmon fillet basted with a red wine reduction;
· traditional game and vegetable pie;
· braised beef fillet with wild mushrooms.

Recipe
Mushroom ravioli, pig's feet, black truffles and foamy broth
by Olivier Arlot, p.264

Muntok pepper is cultivated in Indonesia's agro-forests, a model for the sustainable development of tropical forests. The pepper is mainly harvested in Bangka, an island to the east of Sumatra in the Java Sea. Harvesting is performed manually, seed by seed, before drying in the sun.

NOSE

Powerful salve-like notes of menthol and camphor, with background scents of burnt herbs and enveloping but delicate aromas of leather.

PALATE

Moderately piquant attack with flavors of menthol and eucalyptus.

Aromatic families
Vegetal/Chemical/Animal

In cooking
For best results, avoid over-steeping this pepper otherwise it may taste bitter. Use it freshly ground just before serving.

Recommended with
- crunchy vegetable stir-fry with butter;
- turbot in hollandaise sauce;
- chocolate-caramel fondant.

Recipe
Duck terrine with sake-infused dried pears by Olivier Arlot, p.226

FAMILY
PIPERACEAE

GENUS
PIPER

SPECIES
NIGRUM

BELEM PEPPER

ALSO KNOWN AS
BAHIA PEPPER

COUNTRY OF ORIGIN
BRAZIL

—

AN IMPLANTED AND CULTIVATED SPECIES

Pepper cultivation was introduced to Brazil in the 17th century in the Bahia
region. But it wasn't until the 1930s that pepper cultivation was truly established, as a product exported to Europe
and North America. Today the three main areas of pepper harvesting are Pará, Bahia and Espirito Santo. Harvest
takes place between July and October.

Belem, also regarded as the capital of Amazonia, is the capital of the state of Pará in the north of Brazil, and is the
largest producer of pepper in Brazil today.

WHITE BELEM PEPPER

Subtle, soft, almost sweet notes on the nose, warm scents of herbal tea intermingled with
licorice, wafts of anise and hints of menthol, opening up to reveal aromas of fresh mint and
camphor.

Frank attack, with pronounced tannins that evolve toward discreet hints of aniseed and
wood.

Aromatic families
Herbaceous/Vegetal/Balsamic

In cooking
For best results, grind just before serving.

Recommended with
- free-range chicken with crunchy stir-fry vegetables;
- roasted poultry basted with anise herbal tea;
- veal fillet with gravy and mashed potatoes;
- aniseed-flavored dacquoise with Madagascan vanilla ice cream.

Recipe
Lobster salad, soba noodles, seared avocado
by Olivier Arlot, p.234

BLACK BELEM PEPPER

Soft, subtle notes of camphor bring to mind burning incense, against a delicate and more
floral background suggesting the crumpled leaves of white fruit trees and other more complex, prune-like scents recalling overripe pears.

Frank attack with clean texture. Slightly woody, aniseed-like flavors on the follow-through.

Aromatic families
Spice/Vegetal/Empyreuma

In cooking
For best results, grind just before serving
using a peppermill that allows you to adjust
coarseness to suit the dish, the quantity
required, the impact of the pepper in the mouth
and the desired strength.

Recommended with
- a fried guinea-fowl egg, with roasted white asparagus;
- roasted crawfish, with crunchy stir-fry vegetables:
- marinated red meat stew;
- braised veal brisket, with mashed potatoes.

FAMILY
PIPERACEAE

GENUS
PIPER

SPECIES
NIGRUM

RED PHÚ QUÔC PEPPER

COUNTRY OF ORIGIN
VIETNAM
—

AN IMPLANTED AND CULTIVATED SPECIES

Phú Quôc Island is located in the Gulf of Thailand, some ten kilometers from the Cambodian coastline. The island's production of pepper is today still very limited (see Black Phú Quôc pepper on the following pages).

Red pepper is made by harvesting the fruits when red, at full maturity, just before the berries begin to rot in the bunches. The color of red Phú Quôc pepper is darker than red Kampot pepper (see p.52), with a different method for fixing the red color. The Vietnamese red pepper is harvested by hand, before maturity, then dried for a long period in the sun. In the case of Kampot, the red berries are soaked in boiling water immediately after harvest, then soaked in chilled water.

NOSE

Wild character, sweet notes of pungent, dark Havana tobacco intermingled with scents of leather and smoking incense. Complex on the nose and very soft.

PALATE

Biting flavor, lovely intensity with a marked taste of glazed bell peppers and burnt tobacco.

Aromatic families
Animal/Balsamic/Empyreuma

In cooking
For best results, grind using a pestle and mortar just before serving.

Recommended with
- pan-seared foie gras
  with a Maury wine reduction;
- roasted Touraine poultry
  with cardoons au gratin cooked
  in their own juice;
- baked loin of veal
  in a mildly spicy gravy;
- vigneronne pear tart.

Recipe
Salsify and Jerusalem artichokes,
pepper caramel by Olivier Arlot, p.228.

FAMILY
PIPERACEAE

GENUS	SPECIES
PIPER	NIGRUM

BLACK PHÚ QUÔC PEPPER

COUNTRY OF ORIGIN
VIETNAM
—

AN IMPLANTED AND CULTIVATED SPECIES

Phú Quôc Island, known as the "Emerald Island", is located in the Gulf of Thailand, some ten kilometers from the Cambodian coastline. It has been a part of Vietnam since 1945. Pepper cultivation was introduced here in the 18th century by the Chinese. The island's production of pepper is today still very limited. Some 1.5 tons are harvested per hectare, compared with 8 to 10 tons in other areas of Vietnam. All stages in production – harvesting, retting, washing, drying and sorting – are performed by hand. Most of the plantations are located in Cùa Duong in the center of the island. Harvest continues from February to April. The pepper, known locally as tiêu, is ground with salt, lime is added, and it is served as a condiment with seafood.

NOSE

Delicate scents of freshly mown grass on a burnt herb background, faint suggestion of macerated herbal tea leaves, all supported by a powerful whiff of camphor.

PALATE

Frank and biting attack, with an incomparable peppermint bouquet.

Aromatic families
Balsamic/Empyreuma/Yeasty

In cooking
For best results, avoid overheating this pepper and grind coarsely using a pestle and mortar.

Recommended with
- pan-sautéed crawfish;
- guinea-fowl with crisp (*al dente*) cabbage;
- mint-chocolate fondant.

Recipe
Pike perch, andouillette chutney by Didier Edon, p.256

FAMILY
PIPERACEAE

GENUS
PIPER

SPECIES
NIGRUM

BLACK SARAWAK PEPPER

ALSO KNOWN AS
BORNEO PEPPER

COUNTRY OF ORIGIN
MALAYSIA

—

AN IMPLANTED AND CULTIVATED SPECIES

The Chinese introduced pepper cultivation to the island of Borneo at the end of the 18th century. At that time, there was considerable trade between Borneo and China, via the port of what was then Amoy (now Xiamen). The Chinese imported pepper, camphor, tortoiseshell, cloves, precious wood, etc.

Sarawak pepper is grown in the north of the island of Borneo, and most especially in the part that is Malaysian (the province of Sarawak). The pepper plants are found in the heart of the rain forest, home to the famous orangutans. The harvest runs from April to September, with peak periods in May and June.

NOSE

Dominated by wild aromas of musk and burnt meat, quickly evolving towards woody notes of cedar and sandalwood bark.

PALATE

Powerful attack offering up lingering flavors of wood, with a slight but enveloping acidity that adds lightness to the palate overall.

Aromatic families
Animal/Balsamic/Vegetal

In cooking
Ideal as the basic ingredient in a mix of pepper ground with a pestle and mortar.

Recommended with
- soft-boiled egg
  with sourdough soldiers;
- red mullet or bream
  with a herb basting sauce;
- foie gras terrine with pure sea salt;
- oven roasted poultry
  with a creamy sauce;
- sautéed calf's liver with vinegar;
- rib steak cooked in the fireplace;
- roasted pigeon or partridge.

Recipe
Green asparagus risotto, serrano ham, quails' eggs, truffle by Didier Edon, p.212

FAMILY
PIPERACEAE

GENUS
PIPER

SPECIES
NIGRUM

WHITE SARAWAK PEPPER

ALSO KNOWN AS
BORNEO PEPPER

COUNTRY OF ORIGIN
MALAYSIA
—

AN IMPLANTED AND CULTIVATED SPECIES

Sarawak pepper is grown in the north of the island of Borneo, and most especially in the part that is Malaysian (the province of Sarawak). The pepper plants are found in the heart of the rain forest, home to the famous orangutans. The white Sarawak pepper is made with ripe berries stripped of their covering (pericarp) (see "The colors of pepper" p.20). The harvest runs from April to September, with peak periods in May and June.

NOSE

Dominated by wild aromas of musk and burnt meat, rapidly evolving towards woody notes of cedar and sandalwood bark enveloped in the scent of underbrush-like dampness.

PALATE

Powerful attack, offering up persistent flavors of wood and camphor, with a touch of acidity adding structure but also lightness.

Aromatic families
Animal/Herbaceous/Vegetal

In cooking
Harmonizes beautifully with oven-roasted poultry in a creamy sauce, or grilled rockfish such as mullet and bream with an herb basting sauce.

Recommended with
- soft-boiled egg with sourdough soldiers;
- foie gras terrine seasoned with pure sea salt;
- grilled red mullet or bream with an herb basting sauce;
- oven-roasted poultry with a creamy sauce.

Recipe
Blue lobster ravioli, white radish by Didier Edon, p.214

India's Malabar Coast is the historic birthplace of pepper. *The rainfall and soils of this "spice coast" in the south are ideal for the cultivation of spices. Some 70% of India's production comes from this area! From the 18th century, the English took every opportunity to control this precious food product. And long before colonization, we find evidence of its use in the mummy of Ramses II. Malabar pepper is one of the world's oldest.*

The white pepper is harvested at peak maturity, then stripped of its pericarp by washing in abundant water (see "The colors of pepper", p.20).

NOSE

Notes of sandalwood and exotic wood bring to mind burning incense, intermingled with delicate aromas of green tobacco leaves and chlorophyll. Impressively fresh overall.

PALATE

Smooth texture, quite a bit of bite, with a slightly bitter taste recalling Arabica coffee.

Aromatic families
Empyreuma/Vegetal/Animal

In cooking
An ideal complement to gamey red meat or any other powerful-tasting dish. For best results, grind in a mortar immediately before serving.

Recommended with
· confit tomato and bell pepper tart;
· braised veal chop with sautéed chanterelle mushrooms;
· beef stew;
· a coffee-based dessert such as tiramisu.

Recipe
Pike perch, grilled carrots and broccoli, sweet potatoes by Olivier Arlot p.268

FAMILY
PIPERACEAE

GENUS
PIPER

SPECIES
NIGRUM

BLACK MALABAR PEPPER

COUNTRY OF ORIGIN
INDIA

—

A NATIVE AND CULTIVATED SPECIES

India's Malabar Coast is where we find the earliest evidence of pepper. The rainfall and soils of this "spice coast" in the south make it ideal for the cultivation of spices. The pepper is harvested before full maturity. Drying then transforms the smooth, orange-tinted fruit to a wrinkled peppercorn with colors ranging from brown to black (see "The colors of pepper", p.20).

NOSE

Highly complex first impression. Opens with powerful notes of exotic wood smoke (sandalwood, balsa wood), against a backdrop of delicate floral and fruit scents conjuring up images of an aromatic herb garden.

PALATE

Warm and piquant, smooth but with a tannic edge, exhibiting flavors of smoked meat.

Aromatic families
Balsamic/Floral/Vegetal

In cooking
With its subtly tart finish, this is the ideal pepper to bring out the flavor of grilled dishes cooked in their own juices. Serve ground or crushed just before serving.

Recommended with
- grilled sea bass or bream;
- sautéed calf's liver with vinegar;
- rib steak cooked in the fireplace.

Recipe
Pike perch, grilled carrots and broccoli, sweet potatoes
by Olivier Arlot p.268

BLACK MADAGASCAR PEPPER

COUNTRY OF ORIGIN
MADAGASCAR
—

AN IMPLANTED AND CULTIVATED SPECIES

It was Frenchman Émile Prudhomme who introduced pepper cultivation to Madagascar, at the beginning of the 20th century, following an expedition to Java. He was at that time director of the French institute for agriculture in the colonies, heading up the development of coffee, tobacco and pepper cultivation on the island. In 1899, he wrote in a report that "There have so far been no serious attempts to cultivate pepper in Madagascar, but there are grounds to believe that this liana could be established successfully on most of the east coast." Pepper cultivation started at Nosy Be, an island on the northwest coast of Madagascar, followed by Sambirano. At the end of the 1930s, disease attacked the Madagascan pepper plants, and a more disease-resistant pepper was sought. The choice was the "Belontoeng" variety from Lampong in Indonesia.

This pepper, dipoivatra in Malagasy, is still cultivated on the southeast coast of the island of Nosy Varika at Farafangana in the Indian Ocean. It is harvested twice a year, between May and July and between October and November. There are two flowerings each year in Madagascar.

NOSE

Delivers delicate notes of sweet spice, hints of cloves emerging on a background infused with a whiff of singed herbs and Mediterranean underbrush.

PALATE

Soft attack with an evolving texture that develops warmth and smoothness, escalating into a crisp, biting finish.

Aromatic families
Floral/Fruit/Vegetal

In cooking
A great classic of its type, sure to delight lovers of black pepper.

Recommended with
- oven-baked salt water fish with sautéed scallions;
- braised top rump of beef with spicy sauce;
- glazed veal sweetbreads with sweet spices;
- fresh sheep's cheese with garden herbs;
- roasted pineapple with aged Caribbean rum.

BLACK MATALE PEPPER

This pepper is grown in the district of Matale, a town in the middle of Sri Lanka, some 140 kilometers from the capital Colombo. It is just one of the spices that draw crowds of tourists to the road that runs alongside the famous "spice gardens".

NOSE

Notes of faded flowers with delicate hints of pot pourri and dominant scents of roses, on a warm spicy background showing pretty notes of cinnamon and cloves.

PALATE

Sweet, biting texture on the attack, with powerful flavors of camphor dominated by menthol overtones.

Aromatic families
Floral/Spice/Empyreuma

In cooking
For best results, grind coarsely in a mortar just before serving.

Recommended with
- tomato and bell pepper tarte Tatin;
- grilled or braised red meat;
- herb-roasted leg of lamb.

FAMILY
PIPERACEAE

GENUS
PIPER

SPECIES
NIGRUM

GREEN PEPPER
DEHYDRATED, ROASTED
AND FREEZE-DRIED

COUNTRY OF ORIGIN
INDIA (DEHYDRATED AND ROASTED)
AND MADAGASCAR (FREEZE-DRIED)
—

DEHYDRATED GREEN PEPPER

To conserve the very fragile fresh green pepper and keep out bacteria, it can be dehydrated, extracting the water from the berries. This procedure has been used industrially for several decades, and is sometimes still done naturally by drying in the sun. The pepper obtained by this method retains all of its color, though its flavor is less "green" and its strength is reduced.

The nose offers up powerful aromas of mint and roasted herbs, evolving toward slightly wild notes of Mediterranean underbrush (thyme, bay leaf).

The palate shows a moderate heat and bite that linger in the mouth for some time, with fresh flavors of Vetiver grass and peppermint also discernible.

Aromatic families
Chemical/Empyreuma/Vegetal

In cooking
For best results, grind just before serving.

Recommended with
· roasted turbot with meat juices;
· poached white fish fillet in thyme-infused sauce;
· butter-roasted white asparagus with mousseline sauce;
· soft goat cheese on sourdough toast.

ROASTED GREEN PEPPER

In place of dehydration, the pepper can be roasted. Normally reserved for coffee and cocoa, roasting enhances the flavor of spices.

The first nose is fruit-driven with a minty edge, offering scents of fresh herbs, roasted mocha and sweet spice (anise). Evolves as it breathes towards a touch of citrus.

The palate feels rather tannic on the attack, with camphor-like flavors dominated by notes of anise and menthol.

Aromatic families
Fruit/Herbaceous/Empyreuma

In cooking
For best results, crush coarsely in a mortar immediately before serving.

Recommended with
· spring vegetable flan;
· grilled fish;
· poached turbot with hollandaise sauce;
· beef carpaccio;
· braised veal chop with wild mushrooms.

FREEZE-DRIED GREEN PEPPER

A third technique packs the fresh green pepper seeds in brine (salted water) then sends them to Europe for freeze-drying (dehydration and freezing in a vacuum). Freeze-drying allows a longer conservation of the organoleptic qualities in green pepper.

The pepper shows fresh character with menthol aromas of flowering trees and crisp citrus notes of lemon.

It has a tangy attack on the palate with a mildly piquant mouthfeel a bit like citrus vinaigrette. Highly perfumed overall, with just enough bite to bring out the taste of delicate dishes without overpowering them.

Aromatic families
Chemical/Fruit/Vegetal

In cooking
A whole-berry pepper ideal for infusion – in stock for instance, preferably served warm.

Recommended with
· mixed vegetables with aromatic herbs;
· French green bean salad;
· green asparagus risotto;
· fish (whiting) mousseline;
· poached fish;
· duck breast with a sweet, spiced glaze.

FAMILY
PIPERACEAE

GENUS
PIPER

SPECIES
BORBONENSE

VOATSIPERIFERY
PEPPER

ALSO KNOWN AS
WILD PEPPER, LOCAL CUBEB

COUNTRY OF ORIGIN
MADAGASCAR

A WILD, NATIVE SPECIES

Voatsiperifery is a liana that takes its name from the Malagasy word *voa* meaning "fruit" and *tsiperifery* meaning "plant". It grows on the trees in what remains of the primary forest. The leaves are pointed with oval stems. The fruit is round, three to four millimeters in diameter, with a little tail attached. It grows in spikes on the extremities of the liana.

This liana grows wild on the trees of the tropical forest, in hot humid regions, to the east of the island of Madagascar. The annual harvest, which is entirely manual, is a delicate and sometimes dangerous operation because the lianas — growing up to thirty meters high — are often hard to reach. The fruit is picked from June to August (ten kilos of fresh fruit producing one kilo of dried pepper) then it is sorted and graded by hand. The dark red color of the dried fruit indicates that it was harvested at the ideal point of ripeness, and is therefore a measure of its quality.

This "wild" pepper is often confused with cubeb pepper (see p.94), which is why it is sometimes called "local cubeb" in Madagascar. It has been a favorite with European chefs for nearly twenty years! Voatsiperifery is featured in several traditional Malagasy dishes. It is sometimes macerated in combination with various kinds of chili.

APPEARANCE

Small, shiny, oval berries with a very slender peduncle, mainly dark brown to black in color but with a lighter, oranger shade in some cases. Cutting or crushing the berries reveals opaque, white flesh with a light red hue.

NOSE

Top notes (from whole berries exposed to the air)
Background fruitiness, revealing distinct notes of singed herbs and turpentine wrapped in powerful woody scents (sandalwood and cedar). Leaving the pepper to breathe for a few minutes brings out a candied citrus fruit flavor (citron, mandarin oranges).

Middle notes (from crushed and aerated berries)
Crushing and airing the pepper brings lush aromas to the fore, delivering notes of tangy candied citrus peel and crushed blackcurrant leaves — a flavor very much like fresh fruit marmalade.

Base notes (from ground and infused berries)
With infusion the nose explodes, offering a constantly evolving spectrum of aromas dominated by toasty notes. Ripe black fruit (blackberry, blackcurrant, wild berries) unfolds in a succession of warm, delicate notes before merging into a bouquet of camphor and peppermint.

PALATE

Moderately piquant attack, menthol/toasty notes creating enough acidity and sharpness for a refreshing taste, with liqueur-like notes of green chartreuse reinforcing the underlying sweetness of the peppery flavors.
Good aromatic persistence, very fresh overall with fresh citrus aromas alongside flavors of exotic fruit (bitter oranges, passion fruit).
Tangy, exotic-fruit finish, with more velvety flavors of fresh mango making a discreet entrance. An overall taste marked by scents of singed herbs and predominant notes of menthol. Long aftertaste, with moderate piquancy.

Aromatic families
Empyreuma/Herbaceous/Fruit

In cooking
A very complex pepper, with a tangy freshness that will work wonders for dishes that need a bit of a kick. For best results, grind just before serving, not too fine or you may lose some of the finesse; and never infuse for too long in any preparation, or it may taste bitter.

Recommended with
· crunchy vegetables sautéed in butter, or vegetables au gratin;
· sautéed chanterelle mushrooms;
· broiled lobster with lemony brown butter;
· herb-roasted sea bass or poached white fish;
· oven-baked poultry;
· milk-fed veal rump;
· an emulsion sauce like hollandaise;
· bittersweet chocolate.

Recipe
Instants of chocolate, sorbet, ganache, sponge cocoa cake by Didier Edon, p. 276

FAMILY
PIPERACEAE

GENUS
PIPER

SPECIES
CAPENSE

TIMIZ PEPPER

ALSO KNOWN AS
LONG ETHIOPIAN PEPPER, CAP PEPPER,
LONG AFRICAN PEPPER...

COUNTRY OF ORIGIN
ETHIOPIA
———

A WILD, NATIVE SPECIES

A member of the Piperaceae family, the timiz plant is visually very similar to Piper nigrum in terms of its leaves and in particular the structure of its liana. The edible parts are the flowers formed like catkins, several centimeters long and pointing upwards, unlike other Piper where the flower clusters point downwards.

This pepper grows wild exclusively in the forest of the high plateaus in southwest Ethiopia, 1,500 meters above altitude, and is exclusively picked by the endogamous Manjo people. The Manjo are famous for their knowledge of the natural world, and have been using this pepper for medicinal purposes since the 14th century. Timiz features in all versions of Ethiopia's berbéré spice mixture.

Following the annual harvest, the timiz is dried in rustic fashion over family hearths in their traditional tukul houses, constructed of eucalyptus and bamboo tied with ensete fibers. It is this that gives the pepper its characteristic smoky aroma.

APPEARANCE

A long pepper with fine, oblong-cylindrical spikes of quite rigid structure about three to four centimeters long (roughly one inch), each one bearing tiny berries that grow in a spiral-like pattern. The berries are perfectly round, black to dark brown on the outside with pure, milky white flesh.

NOSE

Top notes (from whole berries exposed to the air)
Peppermint freshness from the first nose, with pungent scents of smoke, singed herbs and camphor suggesting the fragrance of myrrh. Increased pepper/air contact releases a subtle but discernible touch of faded roses.

Middle notes (from crushed and aerated berries)
Leaving the pepper to breathe for a few minutes brings out a more intense smokiness of dark Havana cigars, all wrapped up in fresher scents of damp vegetation that speak of tropical rainforests.

Base notes (from ground and infused berries)
Even stronger aromas emerge with infusion. Scents of softwood show through a subtle and complex bouquet reminiscent of aged liqueurs.

PALATE

Piquant and warm with concentrated, enveloping flavors of burnt resin and cedar bark, and a heat that takes you by surprise. With it comes an impression of sweetness that suggests peaches macerated in an herbal elixir. Powerful flavors of camphor and linseed oil emerge over notes of chocolate with just a hint of bitter cocoa. Good persistence and delicacy, evolving towards more vegetal fragrances of burning wood and incense.
Intense finish triggering an explosion of delicate flavors suffused with aromatic herbs – mint, sage and thyme streaked with licorice and smoke. Amazingly long and crisp, leaving a warm, smooth aftertaste with no trace of a burning sensation.

Aromatic families
Balsamic/Chemical/Empyreuma

In cooking
Timiz has an unusually soft but powerful touch, poised between sweetness and lively sharpness, which makes it the perfect pepper for sweet-and-sour cuisine. To say nothing of its length – the possibilities for delicious pairings are virtually limitless.

Recommended with
- exotic sweet-and-sour salad;
- poultry liver pâté;
- crawfish in citrus *nage* (an aromatic broth)
- *brousse* (soft, fresh cheese) drizzled with fresh herb-infused olive oil;
- bittersweet chocolate dessert with Benedictine liqueur sauce.

Recipes
Roast lamb, eggplant caviar, fennel bulb and coffee caramel by Didier Edon, p.242
Lamb shoulder grilled on vine branches, timiz pepper jus by Olivier Arlot, p.260

FAMILY
PIPERACEAE

GENUS
PIPER

SPECIES
RETROFRACTUM

JAVA LONG PEPPER

COUNTRY OF ORIGIN
INDONESIA

—

AN IMPLANTED AND CULTIVATED SPECIES

Originally from the northeast of India, long pepper still grows wild on the slopes of the Himalayas. Very popular in Roman times, it was one of the first spices to reach Europe, long before the other better-known varieties of pepper. But though it was familiar in the West before Piper nigrum, *its use has now sadly all but disappeared.*

APPEARANCE

A long pepper, with a blackish brown, uniform but quite thin color, arranged in fine, compact and rigid spikes about 4-5 cm long (barely two inches), each one very evenly shaped and bearing tiny, tightly packed berries. The flesh of the berry* is light brown with an orange hue.

NOSE

Top notes (from whole berries exposed to the air)
An immediate impression of pungent notes of sweet spice underscored by heady scents of cinnamon and nutmeg, with more toasted flavors of caramel and chocolate in the background. A few minutes' aeration releases sweeter nuances of zan (candied licorice) and burnt anise.

Middle notes (from crushed and aerated berries)
After two to three minutes' aeration, the crushed berries exhibit even greater finesse, delivering luscious notes of Carambar® caramel and dried tobacco leaves against an all-enveloping background of honeyed flavors.

Base notes (from ground and infused berries)
Heating and infusing the pepper brings out the warmth of the nose, revealing scents of dried tomatoes and sweet pepper. When the infusion turns cold, the pepper notes are rendered even more complex, veering towards scents of fresh paprika and confit bell peppers.

PALATE

Warm and piquant attack, leaving a burning sensation that fades after a few seconds, but velvety for all of its initial bite, with a bittersweet taste of cocoa and roasted chicory.
Sweeter touches gradually emerge, supported by notes of tonka beans and milk chocolate.
Good length and delicacy, evolving towards a fragrance of burnt, vanilla-scented wood and sandalwood.
The delicacy persists through the somewhat hot (burning) finish and remains the prevailing impression after the pepper is swallowed. Burnt notes rub shoulders with chocolate, and the mouthfeel recalls wood tannins.

Aromatic families
Balsamic/Animal/Empyreuma

In cooking
A long pepper with incredibly complex aromatics. Ideally suited to sweet-and-sour dishes but with all the burnt aromas and creamy texture required to stand up to the bitter taste of cocoa-rich chocolate.

Recommended with
- confit tomato and bell pepper appetizer;
- exotic, sweet-and-sour salad;
- rib steak char-grilled over grapevine cuttings;
- beef stew or jugged hare;
- soft goat cheese in a port wine reduction;
- chocolate fondant with Espelette pepper.

FAMILY
PIPERACEAE

GENUS
PIPER

SPECIES
CUBEBA

CUBEB PEPPER

ALSO KNOWN AS
TAILED PEPPER, CUBEB BERRIES, TAILED CUBEBS, FALSE
CUBEB PEPPER, JAVA PEPPER, CUBÈBE, POIVRE DES
INDONÉSIENS, CUBÈCHE, EMBÈBE, POIVRE DU KISSI...

COUNTRY OF ORIGIN
INDONESIA
—

AN IMPLANTED AND CULTIVATED SPECIES

Cubeb pepper or "tailed pepper" comes from Sumatra, Java and Borneo. It takes its name from the Arabic kababa, *and is mentioned in Arab texts as early as the 10th century. There is evidence of this pepper in Europe in the Middle Ages, but it was not until the 18th century and the great European voyages that the plant was generally recognized. The English imported it as a treatment for gonorrhea, for which it was known in India.*

The little tailed pepper seed comes from berries harvested before maturity, then dried and ground. It grew originally on wild lianas, but is cultivated today in various tropical countries in Southeast Asia.

The cubeb lends its powerful aromas to North African cuisine and it has long been credited as a stimulant and aphrodisiac. You still find it today in the Moroccan ras-el-hanout spice blend, in Indian masalas and generally in Indonesian dishes. You can eat it directly, chewing the berry. These days, it is used medically for the stimulation of the nervous system, and as a treatment for certain respiratory problems.

APPEARANCE

Small, round berries with a diameter of five to six millimeters (3/16"), solidly attached to an upright, thin and rigid peduncle. Brilliant dark brown to an almost black color, with a rough, wrinkled skin. Cutting or crushing the berries reveals a small seed with a dark orange skin and a milky white center.

NOSE

Top notes (from whole berries exposed to the air)
Voluptuous character shows with the first whiff, with an array of aromas suggesting camphor, turpentine and burnt cedar. Smoky background, with hints of tea and slowly unfolding hints of freshly squeezed citrus juice. The overall impression is like an herbal infusion of eucalyptus and mandarin oranges.

Middle notes (from crushed and aerated berries)
Leaving the freshly ground pepper to breathe for a few moments releases scents of pine-flavored candy1, honey and mint. A fleshy, voluptuous nose overall, delivering slightly sweet notes of fresh citrus (mandarin orange peel), with a vegetal edge suggesting notes of crushed citrus leaves.

Base notes (from ground and infused berries)
Heating and infusing the pepper serves to showcase the density and complexity of the nose and confirms the hints of camphor on initial nosing. Once cold, the infusion releases a whiff of resin and exotic wood smoke.

PALATE

Soft, sweet, slightly biting attack, with tangy flavors that leave a wonderfully fresh impression of menthol and camphor, overlaid by a trace of sweet orange peel and candied citrus. Good length with a slightly bittersweet finish showing velvety touches of smoke (pine resin). The freshness persists into the aftertaste, with discreet tannins prolonging the dominant note of menthol.

Aromatic families
Empyreuma/Vegetal/Fruit

In cooking
Overheating this pepper will accentuate its bitterness so for best results grind just before serving.

Recommended with
- bo bûn (Vietnamese beef noodle soup);
- fish or crawfish with citrus nage;
- lightly basted, roasted géline de Touraine chicken;
- chocolate mint dessert;
- tropical fruit compote.

Recipe
Géline de Touraine chicken cooked in Vouvray "vin jaune", walnuts and Sainte-Maure goat cheese by Didier Edon, p.248

FAMILY
PIPERACEAE

GENUS	SPECIES
PIPER	LONGUM

RED CAMBODIAN LONG PEPPER

ALSO KNOWN AS
POIVRE DE KOSLA

COUNTRY OF ORIGIN
CAMBODIA
—

AN IMPLANTED AND CULTIVATED SPECIES

Red Cambodian long pepper (dai plai *in the Khmer language, or "short arm") is cultivated in Cambodia to the north of Mount Bokor. It is picked at maturity once the flower spike has turned bright red. The plants are productive all year round, pollinated by the action of the wind.*

It is grown on some twenty small family plantations, in the province of Takeo, a region between one hundred and two hundred meters altitude. The plantations are located at the base of several hills in the region. Takeo is the region adjacent to Kampot, source of the famous pepper bearing the same name (see p.50).

NOSE

Dominant animal notes from first whiff (leather, tanning), gradually unfolding to reveal aromas of honey, bitter cocoa and tonka beans.

PALATE

Warm attack, strong taste and good length. Extremely fresh with its delicate wood flavors, culminating in a very intense, not to say "hot" finish, but with no trace of a burning sensation.

Aromatic families
Balsamic/Empyreuma/Fruit

In cooking
This is a pepper with a lovely mouthfeel that will make sweet-and-sour dishes sing.

Recommended with
- roasted lobster tail in a red wine sauce with glazed potatoes;
- goose foie gras terrine;
- sweet and spicy honey-glazed pigeon;
- roasted hare fillet with sautéed caramelized turnips
- bittersweet chocolate dessert drizzled with a Chartreuse liqueur reduction.

Recipe
Fillet of roe deer, salsify root and quince
by Olivier Arlot, p.266

FAMILY
PIPERACEAE

GENUS
PIPER

SPECIES
GUINEENSE

LIKOUALA
PEPPER

ALSO KNOWN AS
POIVRE DES GORILLES, POIVRE DES ACHANTIS, FALSE
CUBEB, CUBÈBE DE GUINÉE...

COUNTRY OF ORIGIN
CONGO

—

A WILD, NATIVE SPECIES

Likouala pepper is harvested in the north of the Congo, growing wild on lianas that climb the supporting trees to more than twenty meters height. The pepper is picked by the Baaka people, from October to December, in the dense forests of Likouala.

The Congolese call it ndongo bela *or "black pepper". The Baaka traditionally use it ground to accompany game dishes.*

APPEARANCE

Small, round berries of uniform size, with a diameter of three to five millimeters (about 3/16") and a light to dark brown color. Like its cousin cubeb pepper (see p. 94), Likouala pepper is attached by an upright, rigid peduncle rather like a cherry stem. The flesh of the berry is milky white with light green highlights.

NOSE

Top notes (from whole berries exposed to the air)
Subtle nuances of sweet spice (cloves, roasted pepper) punctuated by enticing scents of mace with a whiff of burning turpentine in the background. A few moments' aeration reveals aromas of fruit and fresh citrus zest.

Middle notes (from crushed and aerated berries)
After a brief exposure to oxygen, the crushed berries develop menthol notes of smoking incense and myrrh. More prolonged contact with air liberates subtle notes suggesting a warm infusion of lemongrass and lemon balm.

Base notes (from ground and infused berries)
Heating and infusing the pepper reveals a soft, sweet bouquet with suggestions of dried fruit, nuts and fresh citrus juice. As the intensity ramps up, the nose fans out into a complex blend of herbs redolent of menthol and camphor.

PALATE

A touch of bitterness on the attack, giving way within seconds to a chorus of sweet notes. Velvety texture, with well-concealed tannins that prolong the flavors – dark chocolate has much the same effect – followed by roasted notes suggesting unsweetened hot chocolate. Good length, evolving towards scents of burning wood and incense.
Delicate finish, not too much bite, with an incredibly intense, incredibly long aftertaste for such a relatively tame pepper.

Aromatic families
Spice/Fruit/Empyreuma

In cooking
This is a pepper with a delicately spicy character that will pair beautifully with the great classic sauces featured with some of the dishes in our culinary repertoire. It may be used whole or crushed, withstands cooking and has a particular affinity for olive oil that makes it the perfect pepper when cooking over an open flame.

Recommended with
- traditional vegetables au gratin;
- braised pigeon with a red wine reduction sauce;
- steak tartare;
- roast lamb drizzled with fresh thyme-infused gravy;
- red fruit *clafoutis* (batter pudding).

½

5

3

Anacardiaceae

This family includes around 875 species, mostly found in tropical and sub-tropical regions.

Some of these species are known for their fruits or edible seeds. Mangos, cashew nuts, pistachios and pink peppercorns are all members of the family.

The Anacardiaceae are distinguished by a great wealth of bio-chemical compounds, some of which have a range of useful properties. False pepper trees are a case in point. The *Schinus molle* (Californian pepper tree) produces pink peppercorns and was an important plant in Inca civilization (for food, dyes, medicine, embalming, etc). Its cousin the *Schinus terebentifolia* that is found in southern Brazil and neighboring countries also provided an important resource of plant material for local populations.

Certain species have found a place in horticulture, by virtue of their attractive foliage. The pistachio, sumac, Eurasian smoke tree and Californian pepper tree for instance (*Schinus molle*) are all very popular in gardens.

FAMILY
ANACARDIACEAE

GENUS
SCHNINUS

SPECIES
MOLLE

PINK BERRY

ALSO KNOWN AS
MADAGASCAR PINK BERRY, SOUTH AFRICAN PINK BERRY,
BRAZILIAN PINK BERRY, CALIFORNIAN PEPPER, BOURBON
PEPPER, REUNION PINK PEPPERCORNS...

COUNTRY OF ORIGIN
MADAGASCAR
—

AN IMPLANTED AND CULTIVATED SPECIES

"Pink berries" get their name from the pretty color that distinguishes them visually from true pepper. They come from an originally South American tree that was later exported to Reunion, Mauritius and Madagascar, as much for its ornamental value as for the fruits and their flavor. Common names for this tree vary according to the region where it has been introduced, especially Reunion where it is known as poivre des Bourbon or rose de la Réunion. With a flavor that is slightly sweet and hot, pink berries lend themselves readily to a broad range of cuisines.

APPEARANCE

Glossy, bright red berries with a very fragile and delicate pericarp1 enclosing a black seed surrounded by an oily liquid. Good quality berries should be uncrushed with no trace of wrinkling.

NOSE

Top notes (from whole berries exposed to the air)
Subtle vegetal scents recalling coriander and burnt juniper on an intensely aromatic framework. Crushed blackcurrant leaves intermingled with bitter almonds. Notes of fruit and flowers emerge with air: scents of raspberry and strawberry coulis, then slowly unfolding aromas of small, tart cherries that soon give way to more floral notes – like plunging your nose into a bouquet of wild flowers.

Middle notes (from crushed and aerated berries)
After a brief exposure to oxygen, the crushed berries offer sweet notes of candied fruit recalling blueberry jam. The nose then intensifies, delivering subtle scents of pine resin.

Base notes (from ground and infused berries)
Heating and infusing the pepper into milk or cream reveals still more subtle aromas, as sweet, menthol scents of resinous underbrush interweave with crystallized citrus and the slight sugariness of tangy orange candy. The overall impression is of a heady aromatic blend with good intensity.

PALATE

Sweet attack with a soft feel on the palate, evolving toward notes of turpentine and burnt pine, with an enveloping fragrance of ripe red berry fruit (cherries, Morello cherries).
The flavor is only mildly piquant albeit very intense on attack, supported by slightly bitter notes with an almost tannic taste.
Fine, subtle length gives an impression of menthol and camphor-like freshness.

The flavor of pink berries varies with the production region. Brazilian berries offer smoky, dried-herb aromas that make for a lighter nose and slightly drier palate than their Madagascan counterparts. Their South African cousins meanwhile exhibit a more floral nose, with fresh, tangy notes of menthol and green anise following through on the palate.

Aromatic families (Madagascar)
Vegetal/Fruit/Floral

In cooking
Madagascan pink berries can only withstand the very gentlest cooking (in a creamy sauce, for instance, simmered over a low heat).
They are best off served as they come, whole or coarsely ground, sprinkled over your dish toward the end of the cooking time.

Recommended with
- butter-roasted white asparagus;
- marinated wild salmon or poached fish in a garlic court-bouillon;
- roasted crawfish with sautéed fresh fava beans;
- braised rump of milk-fed veal in its own juice;
- soft, garlicky goat cheese such as goat's milk cottage cheese;
- citrus salad.

Recipes
Red berry pavlova by Didier Edon, p.274
Floating island with a soft heart of red berries by Olivier Arlot, p.284

Rutaceae
Rutaceae

Around 1,900 species are grouped in this family that is found mainly in tropical and Mediterranean regions, though some species establish themselves naturally in the colder climates of North America and northern Asia.

The Rutaceae have glands on their leaves that are highly visible as little white or yellowish spots (see illustration opposite: at the bottom is shown the underside of the pointed part of a leaf, with the little spots representing the glands). When the leaves are rubbed, aromatic molecules are released from these glands in great quantity.

The term Rutaceae comes from *Ruta*, the genus that includes the common rue (*Ruta graveolens* L.). This plant has been used since ancient times for its medicinal properties, and is commonly called "passion berry" even though in botanical terms its fruits develop in seed heads (that open at maturity to release the seeds they contain) and never as berries (which are fleshy fruits that don't open).

Ruta graveolens L. is featured in the royal capitulary *De Villis* that lists nearly one hundred useful species selected by Charlemagne for the royal gardens of his empire. The citrus varieties that are rich in aromatic compounds are the best-known members of this family.

The berries of the *Zanthoxylums*, and especially *Zanthoxylum piperitum*, are traditionally used in China and Japan. Though generally known as "Sichuan pepper", *Zanthoxylum piperitum* is not a pepper in the botanical sense: it is closely related to the orange tree and the common rue, and a long way from the *Pipers*. Once again we find a considerable divergence between botanical and common names!

FAMILY
RUTACEAE

GENUS
ZANTHOXYLUM

SPECIES
ARMATUM

TIMUR BERRY

ALSO KNOWN AS
TIMUT PEPPERCORNS, POIVRE PAMPLEMOUSSE...

COUNTRY OF ORIGIN
NEPAL
—

A WILD, NATIVE SPECIES

This berry is harvested from prickly bushes that grow wild in the Mahabharat hills between Terai and Pahar, above 2,000 meters altitude. It is the basic "pepper" for the people of the Terai, a humid region in the south of Nepal. It is as common in their kitchens as salt.

Once the annual harvest is complete, the berries are dried then sorted by hand (see "Nepal", p.114-115).

APPEARANCE

Small berries, usually split into two parts, with a rather dull, dark brown to almost black color and a very rough rind. The flesh of the berry is yellow-green verging on pistachio.

NOSE

Top notes (from whole berries exposed to the air)
A rather enticing smell of grapefruit and confit citrus swathed in fragrances of limes and combava (kaffir lime), with just a whiff of jasmine.

Middle notes (from crushed and aerated berries)
Aerating the pepper for five to eight minutes brings out sappy notes of candied citrus zest and dried bay leaves evolving towards tea and menthol.

Base notes (from ground and infused berries)
Heating and infusing the pepper releases warm scents of fresh red berries (sour cherries, Morello cherries) interwoven with underlying hints of English marmalade.

PALATE

Only mildly piquant on the attack but distinctly tangy, showing almost sweet flavors dominated by notes of eau-de-vie (kirsch) and camphor. Again, quite floral with a taste that reminds you of Jasmine tea.
Discreet length, with a blend of tropical fruit that confirms the dominant scent of citrus. The finish retains a delightful delicacy, with hardly a trace of the burning sensation you get with some more ordinary peppers. The floral impression is extremely complex – like having a mouthful of suave, velvety texture.

Aromatic families
Fruit/Floral/Balsamic

In cooking
A delightfully delicate, floral-tasting pepper that goes best with equally delicate cuisine – avoid strongly flavored foods. For best results, grind lightly just before serving.

Recommended with
- lobster or crawfish with citrus butter;
- scallops;
- parmesan-crusted fried guinea-fowl;
- géline de Racan chicken with chanterelle mushrooms;
- soft goat cheese;
- citrus salad in a jasmine marinade.

Recipes
Cuttlefish and celery root tagliatelle by Didier Edon, p.258
Chocolate pots-de-creme, grapefruit, limoncello jelly by Olivier Arlot, p.280

ON THE SPICE TRAIL

NEPAL

✳

In Search
of a *Zanthoxylum...*

What first inspired my journey to Nepal was the desire for a first-hand view of the timur berry, a Zanthoxylum armatum of the Rutaceae family. But as encounters led to discoveries, I found that Nepal had many other spicy surprises for me...

Destination Nepal, heading for Kathmandu. A town where you can barely breathe. It's the rainy season. I leave the dampness of the capital, asphyxiated and stifled, and head for the main town in the western Terai region. After several hours on the road following monsoon-swept slopes, I find myself at the base of the Himalayan foothills in Nepalgunj. India is close by, its nearest frontier post just five kilometers to the south. Nepal is enclosed between China and India, a Himalayan mosaic, geographically defined by valleys to the north and south, and its low-altitude plain.

We have to separate the good seed that we want for Terre Exotique from the "chaff" that is for the tourists.

First stop is deep in the local markets, the favorite hunting ground for any spice hunter. A synesthetic experience, and an invitation to travel. In shops and stalls, I smell the soul of the country, I take its pulse, I sense its customs and its commerce, I brush against its richness and caress its flaws, I imagine the essence of its cuisine. I find a refined and utterly subtle powdered ginger, a rare and precious black cardamom dried over a wood fire, delicate timur berries that grow wild in the Mahabharat hills between the Terai and the Pahar regions, a curry with long leaves coarsely chopped and dried... This is Christmas in July! But spontaneous enthusiasm

aside, we must now separate the good seed that we want for Terre Exotique from the "chaff" that is here for the tourists. We must know which are imported products and which are native spices.

It's here that I make contact with the "fixer" who has been my collaborator for the past five years. He takes me to a botanical garden in the Rapti area, where a young botanist called Pandey greets us with an infusion of lemongrass, picked in the valley, one imagines. An elegant courtesy with botanical credentials. The young man invites me to visit a community that is located at some 1,500 meters altitude in a natural amphitheater. Time stands still in this clouded forest place. The houses are lime, their roofs are thatched, the fields are terraced. A lost world like something out of an Arthur Conan Doyle story. Pandey explains that the villagers here are almost entirely self-sufficient. Agriculture is the main source of income in Nepal, which enjoys the sad distinction of being among the poorest countries in the world. Agriculture is critical for Nepal, with emphasis on export to the giant neighbor India.

The Black Cardamom

Cardamom belongs to the Zingiberaceae family, like ginger. It grows in the forests of the rugged hills on the coasts of Malabar in India's southeast, in a region that's known as the "cardamom hills". This fairly rare plant looks very like the Ethiopian kororima (see p.144) and grows on river banks.

A lost world like something out of an Arthur Conan Doyle story...

Each family has its rice paddy, a beehive, one or more timur pepper plants and a plot where they grow cabbage, ginger, turmeric and little hot chilies. Around the houses, peach and kiwi fruit trees grow alongside tomato and coriander plants. Here one eats local produce out of necessity and not just for reasons of militant conviction...

An Exceptional Ginger

The fresh rhizome here is ready for harvesting. It will be dried, then transformed into powder in Nepalgunj, as soon as possible so as to conserve its freshness. Nepalese ginger is very scented and colored in very hot shades of ochre. The rhizome is rich in starch and contains an essential oil of its own, as well as lipids, proteins and carbohydrates in considerable quantity.

Playing the role of pepper expert, I ask lightheartedly: where do I find the "timur ko biruwa kahin tcha"? By way of reply, the young woman who has kindly opened her house to us offers me a handful of the precious Zanthoxylum armatum from her kitchen. I am taken aback by the simplicity and directness of her response. The timur that great chefs shout about is just "house" pepper in family kitchens here.

Now comes the moment to taste the chutney prepared on the spot by our host on a granite slab where ground fresh peppercorns are mixed with chilies, tomatoes and oil. This is a spicy condiment that traditionally accompanies dishes based on rice, lentils and potatoes. With one spoonful, I get the feeling of a welcome that is... very warm in these tropical temperatures!

Those notes of grapefruit and that freshness that is so characteristic of the timur berry are still in my mind as I go off in search of the bush itself that grows wild exclusively in these parts, above 1,500 meters altitude. We cross "jungle" that is typical of Terai, of the sort that might have inspired Rudyard Kipling's Jungle Book. For a moment, this spice hunter imagines himself a tiger hunter... We find the timur still fresh and green, attached to the mountainside in deep forest. It has not yet reached maturity and will not be harvested until mid-September.

Sorting Timur Berries

Once the annual harvest is complete, the timur berries are dried, then sorted by hand. The women sort five kilos a day, working on large woven trays. There are three stages to the sorting: first, the elimination of twigs and other foreign matter; then the separation of black seeds and pericarp; and finally the selection of the ripest berries, based on their color.

FAMILY
RUTACEAE

GENUS
ZANTHOXYLUM

SPECIES
PIPERITUM

RED SICHUAN
BERRY

ALSO KNOWN AS
POIVRE DE FLEUR, POIVRE DE MONTAGNE, POIVRE DE L'ÉTAT
DE QIN, SICHUAN, SISCHUAN, SZET-CHUAN, SET-TCHOUAN...

COUNTRY OF ORIGIN
CHINA
—

A NATIVE AND CULTIVATED SPECIES

Sichuan berries are grown in Asia *and owe their name to their main growing region Sichuan, in western central China. The bush resembles white ash and has purple leaves. The little berries start green (see p.118) then turn red and eventually brown at maturity. They then open to release the two seeds that they contain.*

Sichuan berries (huajiao in Chinese) were valued in ancient China for their combination of freshness and piquancy, their strength of taste and their aphrodisiac qualities. The walls of the "pepper rooms" of the Chang'an royal palace were infused with their perfume. The berry reached Europe in the 13th century when Marco Polo brought it back to Venice. It then enjoyed a period of huge popularity before being entirely forgotten! It was the 19th century before it returned to favor, and became one of the essential spices.

APPEARANCE

Small berries about 5 mm in size resembling a capsule split into two segments, with a rather dull, orangey-brown color and a rough, slightly misshapen appearance due to multiple surface irregularities on the rind (pericarp).
Some of the berries contain small black, shiny seeds with quite a creamy colored, pistachio green interior.

NOSE

Top notes (from whole berries exposed to the air)
Head notes (from whole berries exposed to the air)
Powerful notes of crystallized citrus intermingled with lime and kumquat, enveloped by more vegetal scents of bitter orange peel and kaffir lime zest.

Middle notes (from crushed and aerated berries)
After a few minutes exposure to air the nose develops sweeter aromatics of candied grapefruit zest and dried exotic wood, evolving toward jasmine tea and camphor oil, with a hint of sweet paprika and roasted berries emerging on a menthol background.

Base notes (from ground and infused berries)
Heating and infusing the pepper brings out a warm blend of freshly squeezed citrus juice and fresh red berries (sour cherries) recalling Belgian Lambic beer. The overall impression is one of smoky, woody aromas overlaying jammy citrus fruit and exotic wood bark (sandalwood smoke).

PALATE

Very hot attack, distinctly tangy but remaining floral and delicate overall, not unlike the taste of an infusion of citrus and Mediterranean aromatic herbs (thyme, rosemary). The almost sweet flavors on attack are soon blown away by a fantastic texture that makes your mouth feel slightly numb but without burning the taste buds. Finishes with a touch of kirsch.

Aromatic families
Fruit/Vegetal/Empyreuma

In cooking
For best results, grind the berries finely in a mortar just before serving. Avoid cooking at a high heat to keep the bitterness at bay.

Recommended with
- sautéed green asparagus;
- fine, line-caught turbot, roasted in meat stock;
- semi-cooked duck foie gras terrine (pâté);
- braised beef cheeks;
- molten guarana-flavored chocolate cake.

Recipes
Seared sea bass cutlets, stuffed zucchini flower with squid, béaryonnaise sauce
by Didier Edon p.254
Passionately passion fruit, white chocolate
by Olivier Arlot p.282

Sichuan berries are grown in Asia and owe their name to their main growing region of Sichuan in western central China. The bush resembles white ash and has purple leaves. The berries are harvested before maturity when they turn red then brown as they age (see "Red Sichuan berry", p.116).

Sichuan berries (huajiao in Chinese) were valued in ancient China for their combination of freshness and piquancy, their strength of flavor and their aphrodisiac qualities. The walls of the "pepper rooms" of the Chang'an royal palace were infused with their perfume. The berry reached Europe in the 13th century when Marco Polo brought it back to Venice. It then enjoyed a period of huge popularity before being entirely forgotten! It was the 19th century before it returned to favor, and became one of the essential spices.

NOSE

Wildflower and citrus leaves are discernible in the powerful and delicate aromatics of these berries, evolving toward slowly unfolding scents of lemongrass and kaffir lime.

PALATE

Tangy, biting heat on the attack, leaving an impression of tingling freshness punctuated by flavors of bitter oranges.

Aromatic families
Floral/Fruit/Chemical

In cooking
For best results, grind coarsely in a mortar just before serving.

Recommended with
- beefsteak tomato salad;
- artichokes à la barigoule (braised and stuffed);
- heirloom vegetable quiche;
- one-sided salmon back fillet braised in herb broth with orange lentils;
- herb-crusted rack of lamb with mashed potatoes;
- honey-roasted apricots.

FAMILY
RUTACEAE

GENUS
ZANTHOXYLUM

SPECIES
RHETSA

MA KHAEN BERRY

ALSO KNOWN AS
MOUNTAIN PEPPER, MA KWAEN (THAILAND),
MAT KHEN (VIETNAM)...

COUNTRY OF ORIGIN
LAOS
—

A WILD, NATIVE SPECIES

Ma khaen berries are exclusively gathered by the women of the Akha, a mountain people with an animist culture who come from the north of Laos. They live in the province of Muang Sing, bordering on Myanmar, Laos and China. The main seasonings in Akha cooking are salt, garlic, chili and ma khaen berries. This spice is also gathered and used in cooking in Vietnam where it is called mat khen (mountain pepper) in the Diên Biên Phu region. In Thailand in the Chiang Mai it goes by the name of ma kwaen.

APPEARANCE

Small, star-shaped berries, containing three seeds encased in a light brown pod.

NOSE

Opens with distinct notes of mandarin orange juice and confit grapefruit zest, evolving into subtle layers of lemongrass and smoky Lapsang Souchong tea. A delicate nose overall, enveloped in subtle scents of menthol that add a touch of freshness.

PALATE

Tangy and fresh on the attack, offering moderately intense flavors that leave a fascinating impression of peppery citrus juice dominated by lime.

Aromatic families
Herbaceous/Fruit/Empyreuma

In cooking
In Laos, they add these berries to sauces served with griddled lemongrass, ginger and pimento chicken. For best results, grind the berries in a mortar, either on their own or mixed with cubeb pepper (see p.94) and voatsiperifery pepper (see p.86).

Recommended with
· oven-roasted line-caught turbot, braised with veal and chanterelle mushroom stock;
· oven-baked lobster with citrus butter;
· roasted duck with caramelized turnips;
· glazed pork cheeks with heirloom vegetables;
· chocolate fondant with candied citrus zest.

Recipes
Vegetable Tatin with Sainte-Maure cheese by Didier Edon, p.210
Tonic mojito by Olivier Arlot, p.286

FAMILY
RUTACEAE

GENUS
ZANTHOXYLUM

SPECIES
ACANTHOPODIUM

BATAK BERRY

ALSO KNOWN AS
ANDALIMAN PEPPER, POIVRE SAUVAGE D'ANDALIMA,
POIVRE DES BATAK, INTIL INTIL...

COUNTRY OF ORIGIN
LAOS

———

A WILD, NATIVE SPECIES

Batak berries are picked wild in the north of the island of Sumatra in Indonesia, by the Batak people, also known as the Toba people (population, six million). The berries come from a prickly bush, related in particular to the Sichuan berry (p.116) and the timur berry (p.106). The bush grows at 1,500 meters altitude to the north of Tapanuli and Samosir, near Lake Toba.

APPEARANCE

Clusters of small brown to black berries with a rough outer surface.

NOSE

Pronounced notes of citrus (pink grapefruit, blood orange juice) over an intense background of crushed mandarin orange leaves and more floral scents recalling a bergamot infusion.

PALATE

Soft, almost sweet texture on the attack, with an impression of slightly tangy freshness.

Aromatic families
Fruit/Floral/Herbaceous

In cooking
Avoid overheating these berries to keep their bitterness at bay.

Recommended with
- roasted white asparagus with butter;
- marinated wild salmon;
- fish poached in a garlic court-bouillon;
- roasted crawfish with sautéed fresh fava beans;
- milk-fed veal rump in its own juice;
- soft goat cheese flavored with new-season garlic;
- citrus salad.

Recipes
Seared foie gras in aromatic broth by Olivier Arlot, p.232
Tropical fruit carpaccio and citrus crumble by Didier Edon, p.272

ON THE SPICE TRAIL

INDONESIA

In the Kingdom of the Batak People, in the North of the Island of Sumatra

Batak? A name that rouses the imagination and submerges you in a culture on the boundary between history, myth and legend. It is here in the land of the Batak people that you find the andaliman, growing wild on the escarpments of the peninsula of Samosir. Andaliman is just one of the names given to these little berries that I have come to see and taste and will certainly take home with me, in the hope that they will excite curiosity and enthusiasm in Europe.

After a thirty-five hour journey by air, land and sea, I arrive in Samosir in the north of the island of Sumatra. In Indonesia, "Batak" signifies an ethnic group that originated in Borneo and includes more than six million people. The Batak, also known as the "Toba people", live in communities in the north of Sumatra, in the areas that border the southern and western shores of Lake Toba.

This journey to Samosir is an opportunity to meet the people on whom the continuing availability of these precious seeds now depends.

The "Batak kingdom" is home to a people who were for a long time regarded as "savages". There's a lake here shrouded in mystery that is one of the most spectacular natural sites in Sumatra. Today it's the center of Batak life, and a much sought-after tourist destination. But until the 19th century, Lake Toba was closed to all foreigners, on pain of death if any tried to reach it... Sensational views apart, the generous and fertile volcanic land around the lake represents a real agricultural paradise. Fishing, coffee-growing, fruit orchards and rice paddies all play a part in the local economy.
Having toured the peninsula, I head for a village in

the mountainous areas where most of the Batak live, over 1,000 meters altitude. I find the village chief and explain to him why I am visiting the Batak lands. I am immediately made welcome by the smiles of the villagers and their spontaneous horas ("hello"). The villages of this region are only rarely visited by Westerners, and the arrival of a European rouses friendly curiosity.
I have already imported these berries via Java, known locally by the name "andaliman" or "intil intil" and for only several years called "Batak berries" in reference to the native people. Their aromatic subtlety is something I have come to appreciate, and this journey to Samosir is an opportunity to meet the people on whom the continuing availability of these precious seeds now depends.

Lake Toba

Lake Toba was formed by one or more volcanic eruptions some 75,000 years ago. It is 87 kilometers in length and some 27 kilometers wide, the largest crater lake in the world. Due to its remote location and difficult access, the Samosir peninsula and especially its lake have been spared foreign influence and were for a long time unknown to Westerners. The lake was seemingly a legend until this beautiful expanse of water, which can be crossed by boat, was identified as a huge volcanic caldera. Surrounded by mountains, the lake is now a local tourist destination, attracting mainly middle class and bourgeois visitors.

Harvesting the Batak Berry

The berries grow on spiny bushes, Zanthoxylum acanthopodium, which grow on steep slopes that make harvesting especially difficult. The Batak work from bamboo ladders that they fix to supports. Picking requires considerable agility and care. The harvested fruits are placed in little braided wicker baskets.

On this particular morning, despite the extreme kindness and warm welcome of my hosts, it was hard to forget those bloody tales of cannibalism which have contributed to the Batak myth in the Western world. Cannibalism was once a common practice in times of war and also used to punish certain crimes by... eating the criminal.

In the writings of Marco Polo especially, we see the Batak as ferocious cannibals eating prisoners of war and criminals, while also cultivating and trading in camphor, benzoin, gold and spices. Some historians say it was the Batak themselves who spread word of their behavior, just to discourage foreign intrusion on their lands. It was not until the 19th century that the Dutch colonial government did actually ban cannibalism in the areas under Dutch control. In the course of centuries and still today, the Batak have proved themselves well able to fend off foreign invasions. It is only in the past hundred years, under the influence of Christianity, Islam and colonization that their way of life and culture have changed substantially, while all the same retaining the specific identities of individual ethnic groups. Cannibal myths, traditions and ancestral customs now stand alongside a widespread enthusiasm for social networks. It's a game of selfies on the banks of the sacred lake!

"Do you have any andaliman?"

"Do you have any andaliman?" With every family, the reply to my enquiry was always "yes" followed by the presentation of the berry itself, still fresh, picked the day before, or the day before that. The andaliman is used daily by Batak families, either fresh as it is now (in July) or dried to be used throughout the year. It seems to be the only "pepper" that grows in the region, and is seemingly reserved for consumption in the home. I found no sign of it in shops or local markets, where the stock of spices is anyway generally limited. What's sold on the stalls is white cardamom of which I brought back several samples, a bit of ginger, some turmeric, garlic, onions, limes... and of course, fish from Lake Toba.

The annual harvest is made very difficult by the many thorns that cover the bushes.

Their hands pricked all over by thorns, the Batak compete in agility and resourcefulness to pick the fruit from the branch.

A meal shared on a banana leaf is a chance to discuss the uses the villagers make of this berry, the importance of judging the seed's degree of maturity and the care that must be taken in sorting and drying.

On my return to the village, I am urged to visit Mr. Semunga who is regarded as the specialist in Batak berries, meeting in the restaurant that he runs with his mother where he also gives cooking lessons. Mr. Semunga has forged links with the villagers in the three areas where these berries grow. For the time being, they are barely exploited and only distributed rather informally, but we can be sure that Batak berries would appeal to European taste buds! It is a priority for our mission that any supply line we establish should have positive benefits for the villagers. Never forget that this berry that is so difficult to pick survives only because it is still used today on a daily basis by the Batak.

The families live mainly on red rice and andaliman – both endemic and reserved for family use –, plus coffee. The region is actually well known for its arabica, a cash crop that attracts lively interest, especially among the Japanese who enjoy well-established lines of supply.

The day after my arrival, following an andaliman-spiced chicken curry with red rice, I leave at sunrise with a small group of pickers. We have to walk for two or three hours before we find our first Zanthoxylum acanthopodium and the berries we seek, growing at the foot of coffee plants. The annual harvest is made very difficult by the many thorns that cover the bushes.

Sorting Batak Berries

The fifty or so families that make up the village produce around one ton of fresh berries each year, which yields at most 250 kilograms of peppercorns after sorting and drying. Sorting, which is still a fairly primitive process, is plainly a delicate and difficult operation.

Batak Curry

Fillets of fish are braised in a pot, seasoned with lemon and long red chilies mixed with garlic, ginger and several bunches of Batak berries crushed in a mortar. This delicious curry is served in little mounds on banana leaves that serve both as table and plate. A happy shared moment, rounded off with good coffee.

Pepper Plants and Coffee Plants in Lampong

The journey continued to Lampong, a province in the southwest of the island of Sumatra bordered on one side by the Indian Ocean and on the other side by the Java Sea. More than ten centuries have passed since the first pepper plants were introduced all around the Indian Ocean and most particularly in Indonesia, Java and Sumatra.

In the Agro-Forests

The height of the pepper plants is impressive. Some that are probably several decades old are wrapped around trees up to a height of more than seven meters.

Hayat, our local contact, invites us to visit his family plantation, several kilometers from the town of Krui. You have to walk for nearly an hour to get there. Would we get to see the mythical white rhinoceros or the famous Sumatran tiger? He explains to us that his family has harvested pepper – lada in Indonesian – and coffee for more than three generations. The Piper he harvests grows wild in deep tropical forest, on volcanic land that looks out over the Indian Ocean. Hayat and the other farmers in his district have diversified the crops around their villages to create an agro-ecological system (the agro-forest system, see also "The good seed and the chaff'", p. 12). It's a production system that fits with the surrounding ecosystem. So coffee bushes grow in the shadow of pepper plants that themselves grow in the shadow of large trees and are surrounded by rice paddies, banana plants, papayas and coconut palms. In the center of this ecosystem flows a river. The harvesters consider that it is best to make most of nature and the natural capacities of each plant, avoiding the over-exploitation of the soil that is the consequence of a monoculture. Plants are cultivated as a group, looking to improve the productivity of each one while conserving the natural resources around them.

This is their answer to the deforestation that is blighting the island of Sumatra, where booming world demand for palm oil has led the Indonesian government to authorize the destruction of primary forest for the sake of profit from a monoculture of palm oil palms.

Drying and Sorting

Once picked, the fresh green pepper is dried in the sun on mats laid in front of the wooden houses. The sunlight evaporates the moisture in the fresh, green pepper. After four or five days of drying, the green pepper loses its color and the first black peppercorns emerge. They are then sorted by hand. Black pepper is the main product in Lampong province, being easier to make than white pepper. Care at each stage of production conserves the subtlety and aromatic richness that connoisseurs seek.

Green Pepper and Coffee Cherries

The harvest dates for pepper and coffee are the same, and it is not unusual to find coffee cherries in the sacks of freshly harvested green pepper or on the mats where pepper is drying. The cherries are used in the making of the famous kopi luwak, one of the rarest and most expensive coffees in the world. Kopi means coffee in Indonesian and luwak is the civet cat that swallows the coffee cherries. The coffee makers collect the coffee beans expelled by the little mammal when it defecates, then roast them to make this premium coffee that sells for a fortune.

Harvesting coffee cherries and fresh green pepper requires considerable experience. The fruits must be hand-picked at optimum maturity. The finest aromas come from coffee cherries that have matured to a bright red and pepper that has matured to an intense green color.

GENUS	SPECIES
ZANTHOXYLUM	PIPERITUM

SANSHÔ BERRY

ALSO KNOWN AS
JAPANESE PEPPER, CHOPI, KOREAN PEPPER,
POIVRE DES MONTAGNES, SANCHÔ...

COUNTRY OF ORIGIN
JAPAN, NORTHERN CHINA, KOREA

—

A NATIVE AND CULTIVATED SPECIES

The sanshô berry belongs to the same botanical species as the Sichuan berry. A specialist might detect aromatic distinctions, but there is little difference in the biochemical composition of different varieties within this genus. So while Zanthoxylum piperitum is often the only species cited as the source of Sichuan berries or sanshô berries, Zanthoxylum bungeanum may also be sold under this name. Sanshô berries are cultivated on Honshu Island, in the prefecture of Wakayama, to the south of Kobe.

These berries have been known since the Jomon era (1500-300 BC) and in ancient times they were used to perfume offerings to the gods. They are an essential feature of traditional Japanese cuisine, used most especially to season grilled eels and rare-cooked meat, and they are part of the traditional seven-spice mixture called "shichimi". The Japanese call the berries "sanaho" or "hajikami".

APPEARANCE

Seedless, small, pod-like berries with a short stem a few millimeters in diameter and a color that ranges in fall from green through ochre to brown. These changing colors, together with a rounded shape and tiny pores similar to those on a litchi, are what distinguish sanshô berries from their cousins, the green Sichuan berries.

NOSE

Piquant menthol in the background, delicate scents of lemongrass and ripe citrus to the fore, suggestion of citron and mandarin orange, all supported by Muscat aromas.

PALATE

Biting attack with superb flavors of camphor and menthol.

Aromatic families
Fruit/Balsamic/Chemical

In cooking
Avoid overheating these berries
to keep their bitterness at bay.

Recommended with
· Asian-style sweet-and-sour cuisine;
· marinated raw fish;
· lobster or crawfish tail in citrus nage;
· poached poultry with lemon sauce;
· tropical fruit salad;
· molten chocolate cake with mint.

Recipe
Sweet-and-sour turnip, spider crab meat
in ponzu dressing by Olivier Arlot, p.230

GANSHU BERRY

This endemic berry grows alongside coffee on the high plateaus, between 1,400 and 1,600 meters altitude in the west of Cameroon, in the lands of the Bamileke. The berry is not at this point botanically classified, but it looks to be our first African Zanthoxylum. "Ganshu" is its common name in the local markets.

NOSE

Subtle fruit and vegetal notes recall a blend of citrus juice and Melissa leaves, with a slightly herbaceous background suggesting freshly mown grass.

PALATE

Crisp texture on the attack, evolving into menthol notes with just a touch of bitter orange. Lingering aftertaste.

Aromatic families
Fruit/Vegetal/Herbaceous

In cooking
Overheating these berries may destroy their delicate flavor. For best results, use them as they come, freshly ground just before serving.

Recommended with
- roasted asparagus and sautéed fresh fava beans;
- citrus-marinated fillet of sea bass poached in stock;
- whole sea bream basted with thyme-infused broth;
- citrus zest fruit cake.

FAMILY
RUTACEAE

GENUS	SPECIES
RUTA	**GRAVEOLENS**

PASSION BERRY

ALSO KNOWN AS
COMMON RUE, GARDEN RUE, HERB OF GRACE, SEED OF ADAM,
PASSION D'ABYSSINIE, PÉGANION...

COUNTRY OF ORIGIN
ETHIOPIA

AN IMPLANTED AND CULTIVATED SPECIES

Contrary to the exotic connotations in the name, *the natural home territory of passion d'Abyssinie, more commonly known as the passion berry, is the Mediterranean Basin. Its uses are similar to our European aromatic herbs (thyme, rosemary...). In Ethiopia, it grows on the high plateaus and is commonly found in Basketo country, at the entrances to traditional houses, and within the multi-level gardens that are characteristic of the area. This is the fruit of a sun-loving perennial plant that grows up to a meter high. In Amharic it is called "Ten Adam", or "Seed of Adam", in reference to the story of the Garden of Eden.*

Its leaves add scent to Ethiopian "buna" coffee, and passion d'Abyssinie *is part of the famous berbere spice mixture that is so much a part of local cuisine!*

APPEARANCE

Round, medium-size capsules, attached to a slender, rigid stem similar to a cherry stem, with a bright appearance and a color that ranges from dark ivory to light beige. When ripe, the fruit splits open through the middle into four separate parts. Cutting or crushing the capsule reveals an attractive pistachio green color.

NOSE

Head notes (from whole capsules exposed to the air)
Exceptionally aromatic from the very first whiff, enthralling and subtle at the same time – background notes of exotic fruit with slowly unfolding layers of tea and freshly squeezed lemon juice. A lemongrass and mandarin orange infusion comes to mind.

Middle notes (from crushed and aerated capsules)
After a brief exposure to oxygen, the crushed capsules exhibit a voluptuous nose with even more completeness than before. Sweet notes of freshly squeezed citrus juice emerge from an herbaceous backbone with just a suggestion of crushed orange leaves.

Base notes (from crushed and infused capsules)
Heating and warming the pepper produces an explosion of aromas that confirm the exotic fragrances on the first nosing. Notes of guava and passion fruit are followed by subtle inti-mations of warmth as scents of bigarreau burlat cherries merge seamlessly with a bouquet of eucalyptus and peppermint. The end result is an incredibly potent blend of fragrances.

PALATE

Very soft, slightly piquant attack with a fine acidity giving plenty of freshness. Shows notes of menthol and camphor enveloped in aromas of orange liqueur intermingled with toastier touches of dark rum.
Long on the finish, with a texture not unlike marzipan cake. Other more velvety flavors of tropical fruit (caramelized guava) unfurl slowly, with touches of tropical fruit compote strongly to the fore. Ends with a piquant sensation but with elegant tannins that prolong a long, clean aftertaste redolent of menthol.

Aromatic families
Fruit/Floral/Vegetal

In cooking
The exceptional complexity of passion berries makes them the ideal choice for dishes that need a touch of tangy freshness. For best results, grind just before serving.

Recommended with
· sautéed chanterelle or porcini mushrooms;
· butter-roasted white asparagus;
· roasted sea bass or monkfish basted with citrus juice;
· poultry in a cream sauce;
· caramelized pear tart with orange butter.

Recipe
Tonic mojito by Olivier Arlot, p.286

Zingiberaceae
Zingiberaceae

This family of mainly herbaceous tropical plants includes nearly 1,300 species, mostly found in the Indo-Malaysian region.

The term Zingiberaceae derives from the Sanskrit *singabera*, meaning "horn-rooted". In practice, most of the species in this family feature swollen underground stems called rhizomes. The rhizomes (see illustration opposite) are rich in nutrient reserves and are often wrongly confused with roots.

This family is much used in tropical regions as a source of condiments, medicines and for its ornamental value. Since ancient times, several species have been known in Western Europe, especially ginger (*Zingiber officinale* Roscoe), turmeric (*Curcuma longa* L.) and cardamom (*Elettaria cardamomum* L. Maton). Here it's the seed and not the rhizome that we use.

The *maniguette* pepper or "grains of Paradise" (*Aframomum melegueta* K. Schum.) is another historically important spice that made its appearance in Europe in the Middle Ages. Shipped from the Guinea Coast, this was the source of the ancient naming of the "Seed Coast" or "Pepper Coast", which is today the coast of Liberia and Sierra Leone. In the past, this spice served as a substitute for black pepper. It is very like the kororima (*Aframomum corrorima* A. Braun P. C. M. Jansen), featured universally in Ethiopian and Eritrean cuisine, being part of the most popular spice mixtures in these regions (berbere, mit mita...).

In Southeast Asia, certain Zingiberaceae such as ginger are recognized for their therapeutic virtues. Ginger stands as an entirely distinctive remedy, which is also used in dishes, in infusions or for topical applications, sprinkled on sores or itchy areas of skin.

FAMILY	
ZINGIBERACEAE	

GENUS	SPECIES
AFRAMOMUM	**CORRORIMA**

KORORIMA

ALSO KNOWN AS
NATIVE ETHIOPIAN MANIGUETTE PEPPER,
GRAIN OF PARADISE, POIVRE D'ABYSSINIE,
FAUSSE CARDAMOME, FAUSSE MUSCADE...

COUNTRY OF ORIGIN
ETHIOPIA
—

A WILD AND CULTIVATED SPECIES

Kororima is the common and commercial name used right across Ethiopia for this plant and its fruit — a name borrowed from the language of the Oromo who are one of Ethiopia's most widespread ethnic groups. Botanists took this as their cue when they named the species Aframomum corrorima. It is found mainly in the Ethiopian forests around Lake Tana, and in the central and southern regions of the country (especially in the famous Coffee Forest). It is also found in Tanzania, Sudan and Uganda. "Grain of Paradise" is another name for it, and it has been well known in Europe since the Middle Ages under the name "maniguette" or "malaguette".

Kororima's point of origin is Basketo country, in the high plateaus of Ethiopia between 1,500 and 2,000 meters altitude, where it grows wild under the trees of the Kaffa rainforests. It is also cultivated in the "circular gardens" that surround houses, and in the multi-level cultivations that you find mainly in the Gamo-Gofa area to the west of Arba Minch. Most of the national market is supplied from these two sources (see "Ethiopia", p.146).

The fruits are harvested at maturity when the fruit turns red at the base of the plant. The fruits are then cleaned. A deft stroke of a blade removes the dry matter at the tops of the fruits, after which the farmers say that they are "circumcised". Kororimas from Kaffa are dried in a particular fashion — pierced and strung on a cord of enset (false banana) fiber and hung in the family living space. Smoke from the fireplace gives them a blackish color. You have to cut into the pod to extract these "grains of Paradise".

APPEARANCE

Pale orange to brown capsules, similar in appearance to small, dried figs and containing small, very hard, oblong seeds with a reddish-brown color. The seeds are surrounded by a whitish, dry envelope with a honeycomb texture and reveal milky white flesh once crushed.

NOSE

Top notes (from whole berries exposed to the air)
A powerful but delicate bouquet delivers pronounced notes of green anise and candied ginger and citrus. Evolves towards fabulous scents of tea intermingled with aromas of bergamot and incense. Empyreumatic fragrances emerge a few minutes later, displaying hints of eucalyptus and smoke with just a touch of menthol. The overall impression is extremely complex.

Middle notes (from crushed and aerated berries)
Citrus marmalade on the nose, with more biting notes of lemongrass, lime and grapefruit zest.

Base notes (from ground and infused berries)
Infusing the berries releases suave, warm notes of sweet spice recalling a mixture of cardamom and cumin. Sweeter touches emerge with a few minutes' aeration before yielding to vanilla-like scents of exotic wood.

PALATE

Quite biting attack, very piquant with marked flavors of ginger and lime. Good length, with strawberry in the driving seat, giving the impression of muscular structure with green coffee nuances.
Flavors of citrus fruit and sweet spice on the follow-through, dominated by wilder fragrances showing a barely perceptible taste of grapes (Muscat). Very long and very delicate with an overall tangy-sweet taste.
Quite hot, with an almost fiery edge but voluptuous on the finish with supple, mouth-coating tannins that bring to mind the texture and burnt-herb fragrance of Chinese smoked tea.

Aromatic families
Empyreuma/Herbaceous/Fruit

In cooking
Kororima calls for daring pairings with equally bold-flavored food, having all the tannic presence required to stand up to dishes with a bit of bite. Grind finely with a traditional pepper mill just before serving to keep all of its complex aroma intact.

Recommended with
- broiled red mullet fillets;
- roasted lobster in an anise herbal infusion;
- glazed pork belly with charlotte potatoes;
- soft goat cheese (e.g. French Sainte-Maure cheese with a slice of toasted sourdough bread);
- peppered vanilla bean ice cream with macerated grapes.

ON THE SPICE TRAIL

ETHIOPIA

✳

Kororima, Timiz, Rue... Surrounded by Botanical Diversity

Authors from Arthur Rimbaud to Henry de Monfreid have fed my imagination with images of Abyssinia – the birthplace of mankind. Ethiopia is the Holy Grail for travelers and a paradise for botanists, a "country of aromatics" that for more than twelve years has fascinated me both for the extraordinary variety of the native spices that you find here, and the feeling that this is a place where you can actually read the history of our planet.

This time it was my good fortune to be joined by my friend Patrick de Font-Réaulx. It was our happy ambition to plunge towards the southwest... and we dreamed for weeks of the country of the Basketo... This long-awaited journey commenced in Addis Ababa, the highest capital on the African continent at 2,300 to 2,600 meters altitude. We stayed just long enough to deal with the inevitable logistic issues and establish several contacts. I found us a guide and an interpreter, an indispensable traveling companion in this country that's nearly twice the area of France and home to some eighty ethnic groups with as many different dialects. There are places in Ethiopia where two interpreters are required for any attempt at conversation!

We set course for the Ethiopian southwest, with a first stop at Arba Minch, the town of "forty springs". Welcomed by a swarm of children, we arrived as the weekly market was entering its final hours, in a town entirely focused on preparations for the Orthodox Easter celebrations. Here we are in the main areas for production of the kororima, the little seed that stands as one of the symbolic objectives of our journey. We will see it growing wild at the foot of trees wrapped around with the timiz lianas. But first we see it here on stalls overflowing with spices, and I can identify the characteristics that reveal its particular region of origin. Whether it comes from Kaffa or Gofa, it will be more or less generous and perfumed, so the traders explain to us.

Now we must find the source...

Every family has its rue plant, as we have our pot of mint or basil...

The markets are always an opportunity to find your bearings and rouse the spirits. It's a chance to handle, smell and compare the timiz, the astonishing black cumin, the honey or rather honeys that come from the hives hanging in front of every house, the local mustard, the sublime turmeric, the fenugreek, the ginger, the incense perfuming each street corner for the coffee ritual... I also get to know the most typical Ethiopian mixtures: the berbere that's featured in every sauce, or the very spicy mitmita.

The Timiz

Part of the Piperaceae family, of the variety Piper capense, the timiz liana looks like the liana of Piper nigrum. But unlike Piper nigrum, the flower clusters point upwards. The liana is sometimes wrapped around with kororima.

The Kororima

The fruits are harvested at maturity once the pod at the foot of the plant turns red. Then they are cleaned. A practiced stroke of a blade removes the dry remains above the fruits. They are then said to be "circumcised".

In these parts where the climate is very humid, they are pierced then strung on an enset fiber cord to dry in the family living space. This gives them a darkened color and a marked smoky flavor.

A House in Basketo Country

The houses are built entirely of natural materials. The framework is constructed out of eucalyptus branches tied with enset fibers, the "false banana" whose fruits are frequently used in Ethiopian cooking (to make cakes, flour, etc.).

The villagers have created a model of balanced cultivation that is much studied by ethnobotanists and botanists.

In this profusion of spices, it's the rue (Ruta graveolens) that catches our attention. It is used to flavor coffee, and is known as "passion berry" for its very pronounced notes of passion fruit. It's a perennial plant that you find at the entrance to every family dwelling. Every family has its rue plant, as we have our pot of mint or basil. Thanks to the valuable assistance of Professor Roussel and Zemede Asfaw, Professor of Botany at the university of Arba Minch and a specialist in endemic spices, I also learn how gardens are planned in strips, at different levels. The drier strips uphill are where they grow teff and other cereal crops, bananas, taro, cassava, etc., while the lower, wetter strips close to springs are where kororima in particular grows, in the shadow of large trees. Three cows complete this ecosystem, creating a model of balance that is much studied by ethnobotanists and botanists. The evening of my arrival, I am invited with typically Ethiopian generosity to the Easter celebration that starts at 9:00 pm and finishes at 3 o'clock in the morning. Maybe out of sympathy for my limited liturgical endurance, I was invited to join them at midnight. The scene is a circular church, men on one side, women on the other, all dressed in white cotton, singing passionately for hours on end. The

ceremony is followed by a meal that breaks the fast, featuring most notably the famous injera, a big cake that's a feature of the flavorful Ethiopian cuisine, with as many recipes for making it as there are ethnic groups!

The rain keeps me awake until the small hours, when I am roused by a child bearing aloft a bloody cow's head. This unusual awakening tells us that the rite of sharing the cow has commenced. Each year some twenty families get together to buy a cow to be slaughtered. We watch as it is cut up and shared part by part, offal, tripes, skin... all equitably divided into little piles. Nothing is wasted.

We leave Arba Minch for the Basketo country, an enclosed plateau over 2,000 meters altitude in the southwest of Ethiopia, bordered by Kenya and the Sudan. This isolated area, which was difficult to find on our large-scale map, is a superb region of varied contours. Most of all, it is a place where sought-after spices are grown and gathered.

Here we are far from the clichéd image of desert dunes and underfed camels, which is true for most of this territory. The vegetation is rich and verdant, the land is well watered and very fertile. This is where we find the kororima, harvested in the wet season and strung on enset fiber cord to dry over the family hearth. The time we spend in the heartland of these unique native spices is our opportunity to understand each berry, seed and seed pod in its natural and cultural context. But we never forget that what for us may be a discovery has been part of the daily life of these people for hundreds and even thousands of years. The search for pepper and spices is a lesson in humility, brought home to us by the sheer grandeur of nature!

Gardens Planned at Different Levels

In the region of Gofa, to the west of Arba Minch, gardens planned in strips at different levels support as many as two hundred different plant species – a model of balanced biodiversity.

"Out of Africa", out of this world...

From the Basketo country, we head for the town of Bonga, some ten hours distant by road. This is a land of geological faults writ large. Hour after hour, we pass from 1,000 to 2,500 meters, from 2,500 to 1,000 meters. The breathtaking landscapes display an extraordinary variety. "Out of Africa", out of this world... One moment we are on the savanna with its antelopes, warthogs and scorched acacia bushes just beginning to show their buds. Then just one hundred kilometers later, we are crossing a lush region where the villages have tarmac roads and electricity, there are mechanical diggers at work and hydroelectric dams... rural Ethiopia is transforming itself before our very eyes.

It is night time when we reach Bonga, where we find that all of the lodgings are taken by an official delegation come to inaugurate the first coffee museum — proof that we are now in the heart of the Coffee Forest. This stop in the main coffee-producing region is an opportunity to walk in the mountainous, wooded, humid uplands, where the Piper capense lianas (the timiz) grow close alongside the Aframomum (the kororima).

The return to Addis Ababa is the final stage of a journey that has plunged us into the extraordinary biodiversity of Ethiopia. It is also the chance for a final outing into the "mercato": one of the biggest markets in Africa, and the point of departure for spices that are sorted here then sold throughout the world. I choose the best batches, establish terms of sale with my local agents, fix the price, check the methods of harvesting, the standards of drying, check the transport arrangements...

It will be six or seven months by train and boat before we take delivery of this paradise of seeds. And in the first container that we do eventually receive, along with our selected spices, we will receive several equally unique native papyrus canoes! So we have the means to continue our journey on our home ground in France around Tours...

The Passion Berry

This little metal box is the basis of measurement for most of the spices. Here you see passion berries on sale in the Bonga market. Notice the stalks, seeds and berries of different colors and sizes. The selection of batches and the quality of the sorting are critical considerations.

A young spice seller shows us fresh kororima in the Arba Minch market.

FAMILY
ZINGIBERACEAE

GENUS
AFRAMOMUM
(TO BE CONFIRMED)

SPECIES
(TO BE CONFIRMED)

GRAIN OF PEACE

ALSO KNOWN AS
JUJUBE

COUNTRY OF ORIGIN
CAMEROON
—

A WILD, NATIVE SPECIES

Like the Ethiopian kororima, the grain of peace grows in humid areas all through the year. One place where it flourishes is at the foot of the famous Ekom Nkam Falls (see "Cameroon", p.40). For the Bamileke people of western Cameroon, the grain of peace has a symbolic dimension, featuring notably in the ritual surrounding the coronation of chiefs, and also as a sign of friendship and peace. This spice came to light in a Cameroonian market, and it is widely used in Cameroonian cuisine. After much research, it seems it has now been identified in botanical terms.

APPEARANCE

The whole fruit resembles a long, slender fig, ranging in color from ivory/orange to light brown. The darkest specimens have a hole at one end where they were hung up to dry. Opening the pericarp reveals three loculi, each one containing small, hard, geometrically formed seeds with straight ridges, green on the outside but displaying milky white flesh on the inside.

NOSE

Top notes (from whole berries exposed to the air)
A delicate and complex mix of sweet citrus juice (mandarin orange) and smoky character recalling soot and tar, all wrapped in subtle fragrances of dried flowers and warm herbal infusions – discreet but showing plenty of intensity.
More subtle scents of lemongrass and fresh citrus juice develop with aeration, hints of sweet mandarin orange juice mixed with candied peel evolving towards more vegetal notes suggesting menthol.

Middle notes (from crushed and aerated berries)
After a brief exposure to oxygen the crushed berries1 develop fragrances that bring to mind jasmine tea combined with an infusion of licorice and anise, accompanied by an all-enveloping, intense perfume of citrus blossom (fresh lemon).

Base notes (from ground and infused berries)
Heating and infusing the berries brings out their complex aromatics. This time the nose evolves toward an infusion redolent of smoked Chinese tea, delivering delicate and complex notes that are at once tangy and soft.

PALATE

Sensual and sweet on the attack, marked by flavors of ripe citrus juice and candied cherries. A long and complex taste that gives an impression of softness swathed in slightly tangy hints of fresh red berry fruit.
Bitter notes of citrus zest (grapefruit) on the mid-palate, enveloped in flavors of peppermint. Persistent and long, tending towards flowers and fruit that confirm the nose.
Fragrant but with a soft structure that gives the finish a discreet but intense sweetness with just a touch of bite.

ROASTED BERRIES

Roasted berries exhibit a more intense nose revealing touches of empyreuma, with the citrus core remaining strongly at the forefront but becoming more caramelized (candied peel) as aromas of grilled coconut and toast join the fray.
The palate comes across as softer still, warm flavors of mocha and licorice melding seamlessly with a slightly bitter, tannic core that prolongs the intensity of the taste.

Aromatic families
Vegetal/Floral/Empyreuma

In cooking
The crushed berries will tolerate infusion in cream heated to 80°C without acquiring bitterness.

Recommended with
- Asian sweet-and-sour cuisine;
- roasted pigeon "au sang" (in a sauce thickened with blood);
- game pâté (with lightly crushed seeds);
- chocolate-caramel fondant;
- soft cow's-milk cheese with anise-flavored herbs.

FAMILY
ZINGIBERACEAE

GENUS
ELETTARIA

SPECIES
CARDAMOMUM

GREEN CARDAMOM

ALSO KNOWN AS
CARDAMONIER, CARDAMON...

COUNTRY OF ORIGIN
GUATEMALA

AN IMPLANTED AND CULTIVATED SPECIES

Green cardamom comes from a rhizome-type plant originally from India's Malabar Coast and introduced to North America at the beginning of the 20th century. It belongs to the same botanical family as ginger, turmeric and the Ethiopian kororima. Like black cardamom (see p.160), it prefers to grow on the shaded fringes of woodland or on the tropical forest floor. However, its appearance and taste are different.

Today green cardamom is grown in Guatemala, India, Nepal, Sri Lanka, Costa Rica, El Salvador, Tanzania, Honduras and also in Thailand. Not to be confused with black cardamom!

NOSE

The seeds inside the capsule (pod) exhibit notes of very ripe citrus fruit, with enticing scents of eucalyptus and camphor.

PALATE

Biting on the attack but with a soft texture marked by menthol flavors.

Aromatic families
Fruit/Vegetal/Chemical

In cooking
For best results, grind coarsely in a mortar just before serving – whether or not you decide to remove the seeds from the pod beforehand.

Recommended with
- free-range chicken tajine with crispy vegetables;
- anise almond cake;
- Guatemalan coffee or tea infused with toasted green cardamom seeds.

GENUS	SPECIES
AMOMUM	SUBULATUM

BLACK CARDAMOM

ALSO KNOWN AS
BROWN CARDAMOM

COUNTRY OF ORIGIN
NEPAL

—

A NATIVE AND CULTIVATED SPECIES

Black cardamom is little cultivated and therefore difficult to find. Like the green cardamom and many other species in this family, it grows in the shade of large trees on the banks of streams. It does not tolerate direct sunlight, so prefers to grow on the shaded fringes of woodland or on the tropical forest floor.

NOSE

Black cardamom seeds offer a discreet nose with rather smoky undertones. When opened up, the pods release complex scents of sweet spice, smoked Chinese tea and resin.

PALATE

Quite biting on the attack, with a tannic impression that generates flavors of menthol and camphor.

Aromatic families

Empyreuma/Spice/Balsamic

In cooking

Black cardamom harmonizes beautifully with fish poached in a spiced court-bouillon. For best results grind just before serving – avoid prolonged boiling.

Recommended with

- oven-baked crawfish or lobster;
- plump, roasted free-range poultry;
- white-fleshed fruit compote.

Winteraceae
Winteraceae

This small family includes some 65 species found in Central and South America, Madagascar, Australia and its neighboring islands, and in New Guinea.

The bushes and trees in this family are known for their leaves and aromatic bark. The Magellan cinnamon or Chiloe berry (*Drimys winteri* J. R. Forst & G. Forst) is a species originating in South America that is also sought for its ornamental qualities. The bark of *Drimys winteri* features in the history of 16th century medicine for its use in the treatment of scurvy. Captain William Wynter saved his crew from scurvy using preparations based on the bark of Magellan cinnamon, which separates from the branches and trunk of the tree in rolls much like cinnamon.

FAMILY
WINTERACEAE

GENUS
DRIMYS

SPECIES
WINTERI

CHILOE BERRY

ALSO KNOWN AS
MAGELLAN CINNAMON, FOYE, CANELO, WYNTER'S BARK,
POIVRE SACRÉ DE CHILOE, WYNTER'S DRIMYS,
VOIGUE (IN THE MAPUCHE LANGUAGE)...

COUNTRY OF ORIGIN
CHILE
—

A WILD, NATIVE SPECIES

The Chiloe berry is harvested on the island of that name, in the region of Chile's lakes. It grows in the Valdivian rain forests on the island's Pacific coast, flourishing in the damp, temperate oceanic climate of the Chilean archipelago. The tree on which the berries grow wild in Chile and Argentina is the Drimys winteri, from the Greek δριμύς (drimýs, "acrid") and the name of Captain William Wynter who discovered the tree in the 16th century in Patagonia, while on an expedition commissioned by Queen Elizabeth of England. The berries were at that time harvested by the Mapuche people.

Today the islanders use it as a condiment, calling the berry pimienta chilota because the look and taste resembles peppercorns (Piper nigrum).

The Chiloe berry and Tasmanian pepper belong to the same botanical family and have similar characteristics, even though they grow at opposite ends of the earth — a relationship that traces back to the break-up of the Pangaea, the supercontinent that split some 200 million years ago. These are flowering (angiosperm) plants, both with a life cycle of three years: an abundant crop in the first year, a medium crop in the second year and a very small crop in the third.

APPEARANCE

Chiloe berries resemble dried grapes with colors that range from orange to brown, with some specimens displaying an attractive shade of pistachio green. They have a wrinkled, pulpy skin and contain very shiny, tiny, black seeds the size of a large pinhead, with a bean-like appearance.

NOSE

Delivers subtle scents of fruit recalling the delicate fragrance of citrus marmalade, over core aromas that tend toward camphor with interwoven notes of dried fruits (figs, dates) and violets.
A candied and flowery bouquet develops with aeration, offering suggestions of fig jam with unfolding layers of chamomile-infused aromas that then give way to more flowery notes evoking a potpourri of dried flowers.

Middle notes (from crushed and aerated berries)
A brief exposure to air reveals a sweet bouquet suggesting a mixture of ripe red berry fruit (cherry compote) with notes of confit fruit to the fore. The nose then intensifies, delivering more powerful and slightly volatile scents of aged Modena balsamic vinegar.

Base notes (from ground and infused berries)
Heating and infusing the berries in milk or cream brings out the density of the nose, releasing menthol and camphor notes of medicinal salve that blend seamlessly as an aromatic combination of candied lemon and grapefruit peel. An added touch of eucalyptus makes for a lovely combination of delicacy and complexity.

PALATE

The berries have a soft, sweet texture, with a mildly piquant but very intense taste on attack, evolving toward flavors of citrus and menthol intermingled with notes of ripe red berry fruit (Morello cherries).
The seeds are meanwhile extremely powerful on attack, with a slight touch of bitterness that gives the impression of tannin. Good aromatic persistence, leaving a menthol taste with a strong licorice component.

Aromatic families
Fruit/Floral/Empyreuma

In cooking
For best results, grind the berries over the dish at the end of the cooking time, using the pod (pericarp) or the seeds depending on the desired intensity.

Recommended with
- sautéed white asparagus with a citrus mousseline sauce;
- whole, roasted turbot with "grenaille" (very small) potatoes;
- plain sautéed crawfish with fava bean casserole;
- roasted milk-fed rump of veal with spiced caramel glaze;
- fruit salad infused with smoked Chinese tea.

GENUS		SPECIES
TASMANNIA		LANCEONATA

TASMANIAN PEPPER

ALSO KNOWN AS
PEPPERBERRY, ABORIGINE PEPPER,
NATIVE PEPPER, MOUNTAIN PEPPER...

COUNTRY OF ORIGIN
TASMANIA
—

A WILD, NATIVE SPECIES

This berry grows wild in the rainforests of northeast and northwest Tasmania. The main harvesting area is in the Surrey Hills. The berries are picked by hand from March to April, then dried in the open air. Only five tons of Tasmanian berries are harvested each year. The Chiloe and Tasmanian berries are part of the same botanical family, and possess similar characteristics. Both have a life cycle of three years, with an abundant crop in the first year, a medium crop in the second year and a very small crop in the third.

NOSE

Very ripe fruit notes (cherries, guignolet cherry liqueur) with lovely fragrances of spicy violets, over a wilder core with aromas of old leather showing through.

PALATE

Biting texture on the attack but at the same time soft and suave, gradually unfolding with powerful scents of menthol dominated by camphor.

Aromatic families
Fruit/Balsamic/Animal

In cooking
Avoid leaving these berries to infuse for too long or you will lose some of their intensity. For best results, crush them coarsely in a mortar just before serving.

Recommended with
· sautéed spring vegetables;
· prime rib of beef cooked over a wood fire, with mashed sweet potatoes;
· seven-hour leg of lamb;
· cherries flamed with kirsch;
· Tahitian vanilla ice cream with a Maury wine reduction sauce.

Recipe
Bluefin tuna tartare, raspberries, piquillo peppers by Olivier Arlot, p.224

Myrtaceae

Myrtaceae

This family includes some 5,500 species, all essentially tropical or Mediterranean.

Most of the plants in the family have an opposite or sub-opposite leaf pattern. When the leaves are rubbed, their glands release aromatic oils characterized by a distinct odor.

One species is naturally at home in the French Mediterranean: the myrtle (*Myrthus communis* L.). But the Myrtaceae family is mainly known for its celebrated exotic varieties, like the eucalyptus and the clove tree — a spice that along with the nutmeg tree unleashed some serious trade wars between European powers in the 18th century. We have Pierre Poivre to thank for the planting of these two prestigious spices on French territory.

FAMILY
MYRTACEAE

GENUS	SPECIES
PIMENTA	DIOICA

ALLSPICE

ALSO KNOWN AS
JAMAICAN PEPPER, ALL SPICES, FOUR SPICES,
JAMAICAN CHILI, ENGLISH CHILI PEPPER...

COUNTRY OF ORIGIN
MEXICO

—

A NATIVE AND CULTIVATED SPECIES

Allspice is the dried fruit of Pimenta dioica, *a tree that can grow thirty meters high. This tree originated in Mexico and on the islands of Cuba, Haiti, Barbados and Jamaica. Over the course of several centuries, allspice was introduced and cultivated in Barbados, Honduras, Guatemala and Brazil, before the Spanish brought it back to Europe in the 16th century. It was Christopher Columbus who named this berry "Jamaican pepper", imagining that it was a form of Piper nigrum. When the English conquered Jamaica in 1655, they seized control of the trade in this spice, which then became known as "English chili pepper". The Aztecs were the first to use allspice for distinctive purposes such as the flavoring of chocolate and the embalming of the dead. In the 17th century, sailors used it to conserve meat and fish on long sea crossings.*

NOSE

Shows very intense aromas of vetiver and freshly mown grass, which dominate a bouquet underpinned by scents of green walnut husks and damp bark.

PALATE

Powerful and biting on the attack, delivering toasty flavors of roasted almonds and lush red berry fruit. Tingling texture.

Aromatic families
Vegetal/Empyreuma/Balsamic

In cooking
For best results, crush these berries finely just before serving – overheating may give them an unpleasant bitterness.

Recommended with
- sautéed goose foie gras;
- rabbit and juniper pâté;
- beef stew with fondant carrots;
- chocolate and mint dessert;
- dark chocolate sauce.

Recipe
Beef roasted on the bone, heirloom tomatoes and cecina by Didier Edon, p.244

Lauraceae
Lauraceae

This mainly tropical family includes some 2,550 species, of which some, like the bay tree (*Laurus nobilis* L.), grow in Mediterranean conditions while others such as the sil-timur – that you find in Nepal, Bhutan, India and also China – will tolerate a moderately high-altitude climate.

The plants in this family have leathery, simple leaves, rich in essential oils. The veins that carry the sap within the leaves are very often a characteristic yellowish color. This is a family rich in plants that provide food and seasoning, including some that are widely consumed such as the avocado; also the *Cinnamomum verum* J. Presl which translates literally from Latin as "true cinnamon"; and the Chinese cinnamon tree that produces cinnamon berries (*Cinnamomum cassia* Nees & T.Nees, J. Presl). The latter supplies both its bark and its buds, especially in India for curries, and was already being used in kitchens in of the Roman time. It is very popular in the US and Britain, but less so in the rest of Europe due to risk of liver poisoning if too much is eaten. The bark of "true" cinnamon (*Cinnamomum verum*) is often used instead.

GENUS	SPECIES
LINDERA	NEESIANA

SIL-TIMUR BERRY

ALSO KNOWN AS
KATHMANDU PEPPER

COUNTRY OF ORIGIN
NEPAL
—

A WILD, NATIVE SPECIES

The sil-timur comes from a deciduous bush, growing at between 1,200 and 2,700 meters altitude in Himalayan and sub-tropical Asia, especially in the Nepalgunj region in southwest Nepal. It flowers between October and November, depending on the region. The berries are picked by hand.

The Nepalese use these berries liberally as seasoning, crushed in a mortar, then added to a vegetable soup or plate of rice. You will find sil-timur at all the stalls in local markets (see "Nepal", p.108).

NOSE

Delicate notes of very ripe citrus recalling blood oranges and pink grapefruit, over a core infused with soft, herbal scents, lemon balm intermingling with lemongrass.

PALATE

Soft texture on the attack, evolving towards warm, suave notes of candied citrus offset by a touch of freshness from a slightly bitter, roasted finish.

Aromatic families
Fruit/Herbaceous/Empyreuma

In cooking
For best results, grind coarsely over your dish just before serving.

Recommended with
- butter-baked fish with a lemony basting sauce;
- creamy poultry breast with garden herbs;
- rack of lamb with a concentrated thyme sauce;
- tropical fruit puree.

Recipe
Bay scallops, duck, Autumn sun by Didier Edon, p.218

GENUS		SPECIES
CINNAMOMUM		CASSIA

CINNAMON BERRY

ALSO KNOWN AS
CHINESE CASSIA, CHINESE CINNAMON, CANNELIER CASSE,
CANNELLE DE COCHINCHINE, FALSE CINNAMON...

COUNTRY OF ORIGIN
CHINA
———

AN IMPLANTED AND CULTIVATED SPECIES

The cinnamon that we know best comes as pieces of bark, and this is what we mostly use in our kitchens. In practice, there are no fewer than five different species of the genus Cinnamomum that may provide this bark, of which Cinnamomum cassia, which has been known since ancient times, is one of the most used for its aromatic qualities. We also use the buds of this species, known as "cinnamon berries".

NOSE

Delivers powerful aromas of cloves and roasted coffee, complemented by notes of dark tobacco smoke and cocoa.

PALATE

Warm and biting on the attack, leaving an aftertaste that is soft and sweet but also slightly bitter with its marked hints of roasted walnuts.

Aromatic families
Spice/Empyreuma/Fruit

In cooking
For best results, "cinnamon berries" should be finely ground just before serving – a pepper grinder is a nice easy way to revisit the use of cinnamon in cooking.

Recommended with
· cauliflower mousse;
· sautéed foie gras, basted with a banyuls sweet wine reduction;
· apple and pear salted butterscotch tart;
· crème anglaise (homemade custard) with gingerbread.

Recipe
Squab, figs and pastilla
by Didier Edon, p.238

Annonaceae

Annonaceae

Around 2,100 species are included in this pan-tropical family, mainly found in the African and Asiatic tropics.

The Annonaceae are characterized by the richness of their aromatic compounds, most evident in a species like the ylang-ylang or, among the spices, the grains of Selim (*Xylopia aethiopica* [Dunal] A. Rich or Kili). This medicinal plant is used to treat dysentery and bronchial infections as well as certain ophthalmic conditions. Its aromatic composition also protects wood against termite attack. Another species of Annonaceae, grains of Kili, are highly acclaimed in Senegal where they are one of the ingredients in the famous café touba.

FAMILY
ANNONACEAE

GENUS	SPECIES
XYLOPIA	AETHIOPICA

GRAINS OF SELIM

ALSO KNOWN AS
KILI, BLACK CHILI, GUINEA PEPPER, NGANI-KOUN...

COUNTRY OF ORIGIN
BENIN
—

A NATIVE SPECIES

This species is found in central and western Africa, where the seeds from the dried seed heads are very popular for their aromatic qualities.

NOSE

Develops notes of menthol and turpentine, complemented by a mixture of smoked herbs plus touches of bitter cocoa and lemongrass.

PALATE

Moderately piquant, characterized by a dash of musky, wild spice.

Aromatic families
Vegetal/Empyreuma/Balsamic

In cooking
For best results, grind the seeds in a mortar just before serving.

Recommended with
- braised sea bass fillet on a bed of crispy cabbage;
- roasted veal rump with carrot and thyme puree;
- glazed veal shank with seasonal vegetables;
- sautéed calf's liver basted with a red wine and vinegar reduction sauce.

Recipe
Filet mignon of veal, veal sweetbread cannelloni, mushrooms by Didier Edon, p.246

Apiaceae
Apiaceae

This family is represented on every continent and includes some 3,500 species. Members of the family are essentially herbaceous plants as well as several bushes.

Most of the herbaceous plants are distinguished by leaves that are cut away in an often delicate pattern.

The Apiaceae are frequently used for the aromatic richness of their leaves, roots, seeds, resins, etc. In Europe, the most commonly consumed species include the carrot, celery, chervil, parsley and angelica. The alexander is another that is less well known but was widely used in the Middle Ages. It featured notably in the *De Villis* capitulary that Charlemagne circulated in Western Europe listing the plant species that he wanted grown in his royal gardens.

GENUS	SPECIES
CORIANDRUM	SATIVUM

CORIANDER (SEEDS)

ALSO KNOWN AS
ARAB PARSLEY, CHINESE PARSLEY...

COUNTRY OF ORIGIN
SPAIN
—

AN IMPLANTED AND CULTIVATED SPECIES

Coriander grows in most temperate regions of the world, so successfully that its natural point of origin remains uncertain to this day. We can all the same be sure that this aromatic plant has been cultivated for a very long time. We have even found traces of it on ancient Egyptian papyrus!

NOSE

Subtle notes of fresh citrus up front, mandarin orange juice over a flowery core of green anise and fennel.

PALATE

Supple and delicate attack, wonderfully fragrant with flavors of lime and camphor and a touch of wood on the finish.

Aromatic families
Fruit/Herbaceous/Vegetal

In cooking
For best results, crush coriander seeds just before serving – don't overheat or you will bring out the seeds' grassy, herbaceous side.

Recommended with
- sautéed crawfish with grapefruit zest;
- sea bream seasoned with citrus vinaigrette;
- roasted baby lamb;
- sweet spice cake.

Recipe
Cancale oysters in escabeche, coriander seeds by Olivier Arlot, p.220

GENUS	SPECIES
SMYRNIUM	OLUSATRUM

ALEXANDERS

ALSO KNOWN AS
ALISANDERS, HORSE PARSLEY, SMYRNIUM, BLACK LOVAGE,
MACEDONIA PARSLEY, WILD CELERY, POIVRE DE L'ILE DE RÉ,
POIVRE DES MOINES...

COUNTRY OF ORIGIN
FRANCE
—

AN IMPLANTED AND WILD SPECIES

This species was once common and cultivated, but it has become rather forgotten today. Many parts of the plant are edible: the tuber root, the stems, the leaves, the seeds, etc. It originally grew wild around the Mediterranean basin, in coastal positions especially. Then it came to be grown as a crop in many northern European countries and so became much more widespread. In France, its cultivation is recorded on the Ile de Ré where it was grown by the Cistercian monks of the Abbaye des Châteliers. Hardly surprising given its reputation for suppressing "masculine urges", which led to its distribution among the monasteries... Alexanders today grows typically on the fringes of salt marshes.

NOSE

An exquisitely delicate and subtle bouquet, dominated by surprising scents of truffles complemented by an anise-like fragrance of cooked fennel.

PALATE

Subtle notes up front, lemony but not very piquant with a long, smooth aftertaste.

Aromatic families
Fruit/Empyreuma/Herbaceous

In cooking
For best results, crush in a mortar just before serving – infusing in cream will bring out the flavor of Alexanders.

Recommended with
· crispy fried vegetables;
· asparagus with hollandaise sauce;
· mashed potatoes and celery;
· veal chop with cream;
· roasted sea bass.

Recipe
Veal grendadins, tajine-style
by Olivier Arlot, p.262

Cupressaceae

Cupressaceae

This family of conifers includes around 130 species, among them the famous giant Californian sequoias and others among our most long-living trees.

The juniper tree (*Juniperus communis* L.) has fleshy cones that can be used in cooking, but are mistakenly called Juniper "berries". Their structure is in fact comparable to pine cones with seeds inside (see *Juniperus* illustration opposite) and they are not at all berries in the botanical sense of the term. The Juniper is one of the very few conifers that have any part to play in the human diet.

```
┌─────────────────────────────────────────────┐
│                                             │
│                  FAMILY                     │
│               CUPRESSACEAE                  │
│  ─────────────────────────────────────────  │
│      GENUS         │        SPECIES         │
│    JUNIPERUS       │       COMMUNIS         │
│  ─────────────────────────────────────────  │
│                                             │
│            JUNIPER BERRY                    │
│                                             │
│                ALSO KNOWN AS                │
│ COMMON JUNIPER, JUNIPER, PETERON, PETROT... │
│  ─────────────────────────────────────────  │
│              COUNTRY OF ORIGIN              │
│                  ALBANIA                    │
│                    ──                       │
│                                             │
│       A NATIVE AND CULTIVATED SPECIES       │
│                                             │
└─────────────────────────────────────────────┘
```

Despite what the popular name suggests, this is not a berry in the botanical sense, *but a fleshy conifer cone — and a strange pinecone at that. It takes two years for the cone to grow to maturity, starting green and darkening as it ripens, displaying attractive bluish tones as it acquires an aromatic richness and complexity that is unique among conifer cones.*

NOSE

Wild, almost musky notes recall the pungent smell of resinous underbrush, woodland scents of humus and wild mushrooms evolving with a little aeration into notes of damp leather.

PALATE

Moderately biting texture on the attack but with a creamy, almost sweet taste and a touch of wood on the finish.

Aromatic families

Animal/Vegetal/Spice

In cooking

Infusing whole juniper berries liberates powerful balsamic scents showing hints of camphor and turpentine.

Recommended with

- white fish cooked in a court-bouillon infused with juniper berries;
- jugged venison (made with the meat of a female deer);
- roast haunch of wild boar.

Lamiaceae

Lamiaceae

This family is represented on every continent and includes some 6,500 species of herb, bush and tree.

The Lamiaceae include many aromatic herbs and are widely represented in our gardens (mint, lemon balm, sage, thyme, rosemary, lavender, etc.). They also often provide essential oils. The chaste tree or monk's pepper (*Vitex agnus-castus* L.), which is widely used today in horticulture, was used in the Middle Ages to suppress sexual impulses in the monasteries. It is this therapeutic – or moral! – property that has earned these fruits their popular name of "monk's pepper". They are used in cooking for their abundance of aromatic molecules.

FAMILY
LAMIACEAE

GENUS	SPECIES
VITEX	AGNUS-CASTUS

MONK'S PEPPER

ALSO KNOWN AS
VITEX, CHASTE TREE, CHASTEBERRY, ABRAHAM'S BALM,
LILAC CHASTETREE, POIVRE SAUVAGE, PETIT POIVRE,
POIVRE DU PARADIS...

COUNTRY OF ORIGIN
MOROCCO
—

A NATIVE AND CULTIVATED SPECIES

Monk's pepper is one of the rare species of Vitex to become established in the Mediterranean area. Most varieties occur in tropical regions. It is as much known for its aphrodisiac properties as for its anti-aphrodisiac qualities, no doubt depending on the dose. There has yet to be any definitive medical proof on the matter. The seeds, leaves and young stems are sometimes consumed as a form of ethno-medicine, but the most aromatic parts are the seeds.

NOSE

Floral and roasted notes recall delicate scents of an infusion of aromatic herbs intermingled with notes of faded roses. Subtle floral touches emerge after a few moments of aeration.

PALATE

Sweet and suave texture on the attack, showing a mixture of powerful notes of camphor and menthol-dominated character.

Aromatic families
Spice/Oxidative/Vegetal

In cooking
For best results, crush coarsely just before serving.

Recommended with
- broiled line-caught bass with fennel;
- oven-roasted poultry, basted with a reduction sauce;
- rib eye steak cooked on a charcoal grill.

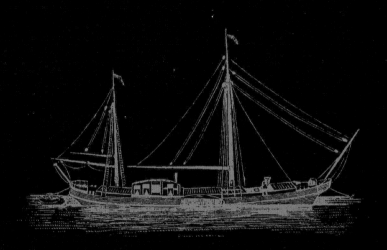

The Adventure Continues ...

Man has been using spices for over 6,000 years, and yet, even today, they are the object of research and new discoveries.

Whether native or implanted or cultivated, spices do move from place to place, spreading out from their points of origin to become an established part of civilizations, sought after for their particular qualities and their special flavors.

Ours is a passionate and demanding quest, working alongside the producers and their cultures. In return we are rewarded with some remarkable encounters, with humankind and plant life alike. In the local market, in a tropical forest or deep in a valley — the "pepper ferryman" is ever alert for new plants, aware of each seductive perfume, quick to spot any uses that are new to him... It is hard to say exactly where our journey started and we certainly do not know where it will end. Varying climatic conditions, botanical diversity and cultural richness are a continual reminder that we should not over-estimate our progress.

A little-known fruit, a name with an exotic ring to it, an unidentified flavor — the adventure continues...

```
┌─────────────────────────────────────────┐
│                 FAMILY                    │
│                   ?                       │
│  ───────────────────────────────────────  │
│     GENUS              SPECIES            │
│       ?          │        ?               │
│  ───────────────────────────────────────  │
│                                           │
│         MALAM  BERRY                      │
│                                           │
│  ───────────────────────────────────────  │
│                                           │
│           COUNTRY OF ORIGIN               │
│              CAMEROON                      │
│                 ───                       │
│                                           │
│             SPECIES ?                     │
└─────────────────────────────────────────┘
```

We unearthed malam in the market in Loum, a city in the west of Cameroon — and this spice is still an enigma. Its botanical identification and origin remain a mystery. We are deep in the quest, on a trail without end...

The gastronomy of Cameroon is as rich and varied as its population, with some 250 distinct ethnic groups! Cameroonian cuisine is built on hearty and highly spiced dishes, and malam is plainly in daily use, in all kinds of sauces. It has a natural place in our story.

NOSE

Tends towards overripe notes of fruit and smoke, bringing to mind a delicate mélange of pitted red fruits with fragrant spice peeking through.

PALATE

Moderately biting texture on the attack, but at the same time suave and nicely tempered by subtle flavors of menthol and camphor.

Aromatic families
Fruit/Balsamic/Empyreuma

In cooking
For best results, crush coarsely in a mortar just before serving.
To make a mixture of spices "Cameroon-style", as used by Marie Penja for her famous "DG" chicken (see "Cameroon" p.40), take a handful of traditional spices (malam, rondelle, pébé, essesse, njansang, etc.) and place them on a grinding stone. Now take a polished stone and pound them to a powder using and a bit of elbow grease. The local women then knead this mix into a paste (the oily varieties such as njansang act as binders) ready for use in dishes of every description. The precise ratio of ingredients and blend of flavors is a well-kept secret that has been passed down through generations.

Recommended with
- oven-baked saltwater fish basted with veal stock;
- beef cheeks braised in Chinon wine;
- sautéed cherries in a port wine reduction.

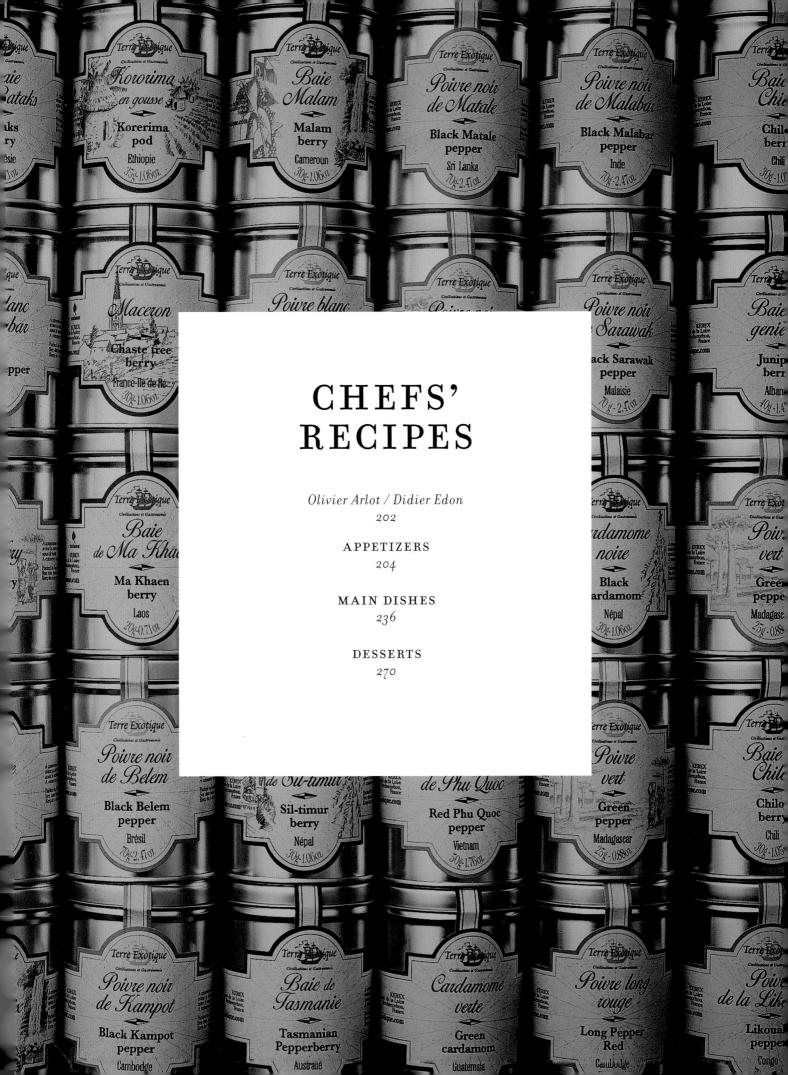

CHEFS' RECIPES

Olivier Arlot

Chef of Olivier Arlot Restaurant, Le Bistro and L'Atelier

— *Olivier Arlot's Recipes* —

A lively, determined man in his thirties, Olivier Arlot has experienced the glamour, fire and rush of the greatest kitchen teams led by the most talented chefs: Michel del Burgo at Taillevent, Jean-François Piège at the Plaza Athénée, then at the Crillon (all in Paris); Jean-Marc Delacourt at La Chèvre d'Or (in Provence), Jean-François Rouquette at the Vendôme Park Hyatt in Paris… From all these experiences, he learned the high quality standards, rigor and technical mastery required from a chef by French culinary tradition.

In 2008, he left the world of luxury hotels and decided to return to his native region of Touraine. That is where he opened his first restaurant in Tours, to sell it later in 2011. That same year, the young chef took over La Chancelière, an authentic local institution to which he conveyed his own personal style and youthful energy. Busy, challenge-loving Olivier Arlot did not stop there, opening his Bistro in 2015, then L'Atelier in 2016. Surrounded by a twenty-strong, trustworthy kitchen team to which he communicates his passion and energy, Olivier — once described by the Gault&Millau guide as "one of tomorrow's great chefs" — appears to have fulfilled his mission.

"I like my cooking to be simple", he says, "and based on excellent products. I want people to be able to identify what is on their plate." Both restrained and creative, streamlined and balanced, his market-sourced cooking shows his deep respect for natural ingredients and his wish not to betray them. A precise cook, he likes to enhance and magnify taste. His slash-studded menus, quite in the style of his generation, are a promise of exhilarating taste pairings, strictly measured cooking and a very balanced sense of seasoning. Spices, likewise, are used in the same painstaking manner. He enjoys sprinkling his dishes with a dash of freshly ground Sarawak pepper, but also, depending on his mood, mixing in a little fleur de sel and Sichuan berries, or crushing some fresh herbs and a few grains of sanshô pepper at the last minute to perk up a meat or seafood dish. Not to forget, of course, the Passion berry, which he just discovered and whose charms he is only beginning to explore…

Didier Edon

Chef of Domaine des Hautes Roches in Rochecorbon

Trained in the most splendid restaurants of France — particularly at L'Aigle Noir in Fontainebleau, then at the Château de Marçay, near Chinon — with a few escapes to Courchevel and Saint-Tropez, Didier Edon has found in Le Domaine des Hautes Roches a perfect, tufa-carved showcase for his unique talent.

The restaurant, which he has been managing since 1989 with his wife Christine, is an inspirational setting for his refined gastronomic cuisine, which is precise, generous, timeless and creative — just like him. A style he tries to convey to his youthful kitchen team. In 1990, the half-troglodyte house built above the Vouvray vineyards was graced with a Michelin star, which he temporarily lost, then recovered in 1998.

Born in Saint-Nazaire — a city which historically lies at the border of two regions, Brittany and the Nantes country —, Didier Edon navigates between the cooking traditions of Touraine and those of Brittany, leaning decidedly towards marine flavors.

A man of stylish gestures, of pristine ingredients, he likes to mention his best suppliers by their full names. "People should retrain themselves to eat every bit of an animal", he points out. Indeed, one can eat every part of a pig, but the same can be said of the Breton lobster, which he stuffs into delightful ravioli, seasoned with white Sarawak pepper. On the subject of pepper, Didier Edon discovered its many varieties through Erwan de Kerros, from whom he got his passion for Penja peppercorns, which he now uses on a daily basis. "From the ubiquitous mignonnette", he remembers, "to routine turns of pepper mill, pepper was sprinkled onto our plates as if by reflex. We had forgotten that we could use all sorts of pepper, or use a mortar…" Salt may be a taste enhancer, but this chef loves to bring out the beauty of a dish with a few grains of pepper. Like wines, pepper gives access to all sorts of pairings. His latest crush is Nepalese timur pepper, whose citrus notes awake the tastebuds of Les Hautes Roches' fortunate guests.

— Didier Edon's Recipes —

APPETIZERS

GREEN PENJA PEPPERCORNS IN BRINE

Mackerel Fillets
and Rillettes on Toast

PREPARATION TIME	COOKING TIME
20 MINUTES	7–10 MINUTES
MARINATING TIME	DRYING TIME
10 MINUTES	ABOUT 1 HOUR
	(PREFERABLY 1 DAY AHEAD)

SERVES 4

**FOR THE MACKEREL
(FILLETS AND RILLETTES)**

*4 slices sandwich bread,
crusts removed*

4 boneless mackerel fillets

Juice of 1 lemon

Olive oil

1 tsp green peppercorns in brine

1 tbsp heavy cream

½ shallot

A few leaves of tarragon

1 egg yolk

½ tsp Dijon mustard

TO SERVE

4 cherry tomatoes

2 scallions

2 baby fennel bulbs

4 quail's eggs, hard-boiled

4 leaves from a lettuce heart

Olive oil

Salt, Penja peppercorns in brine

THE MACKEREL FILLETS AND RILLETTES

Preheat the oven to 350 °F (gas mark 6).

Lay the sliced bread on a baking sheet and put it in the oven for 1 minute until dried and slightly browned. While the slices are still hot, lay them on a rolling pin for about 1 hour to give them a curved shape.

Put the mackerel fillets in a deep dish and marinate them with the lemon juice for 2 minutes, then halve each fillet, separating the tail end from the head end. Remove the tail ends from the marinade and set them aside. Pour a little olive oil onto the head ends and sprinkle them with 1 pinch of salt. Marinate for 8 minutes, then peel off the skin.

Make the mackerel rillettes: rinse the green peppercorns in clear water, then chop them with a knife. Using a fork, mash the marinated head ends of the mackerel fillets. Stir in 1/2 tsp of chopped green peppercorns; stir in the cream.

Peel the shallot and chop it finely. Chop the tarragon. Put the egg yolk and mustard in a bowl and beat them into a mayonnaise while adding the olive oil gradually. Add the tarragon, shallot and remaining green peppercorns.

TO SERVE

Slice the cherry tomatoes, scallions and raw baby fennel bulbs. Peel the quail's eggs and cut them into 4.

Lay a curved slice of toast on each plate. Lay the lettuce, sliced tomatoes, scallions, baby fennel and quail's eggs. Cover with the marinated mackerel fillet and a spoonful of mackerel rillettes. Sprinkle with a few drops of olive oil and a tablespoonful of green peppercorn mayonnaise.

The bread may be dried in the oven 1 day ahead.

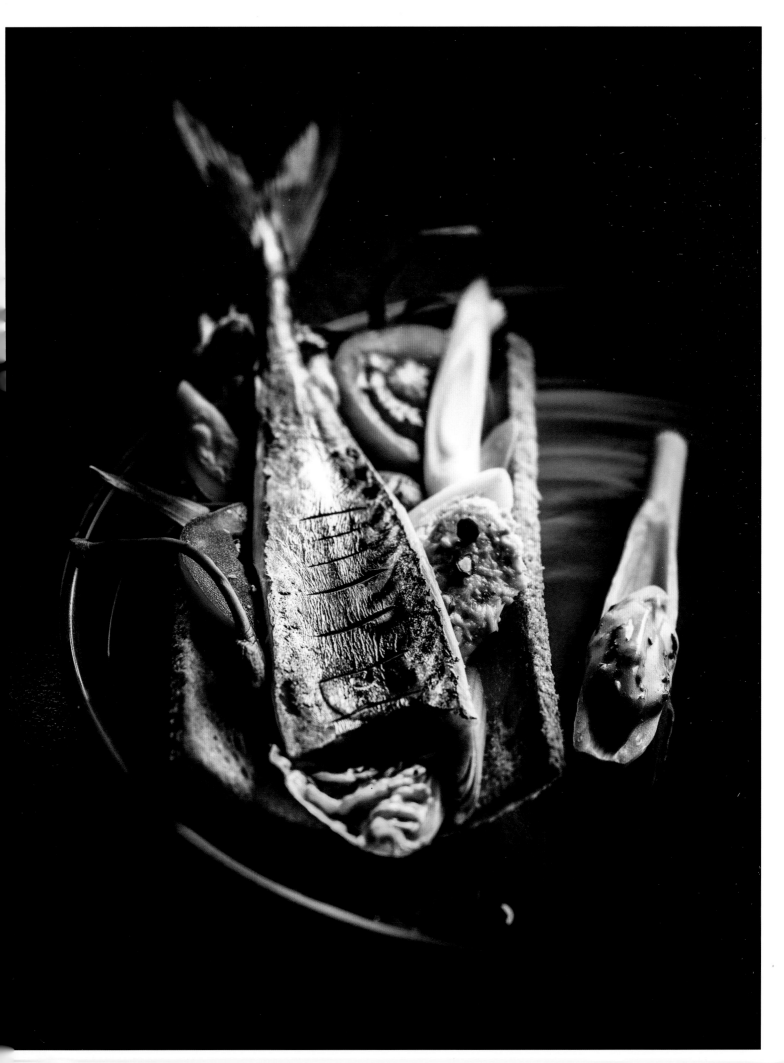

Pressed Veal Sweetbreads,
Salmon, Artichoke

PREPARATION TIME	COOKING TIME
45 MINUTES	40–45 MINUTES
	(if the artichokes are fresh)

SERVES 4

FOR THE BRAISED VEAL SWEETBREADS

½ carrot

½ onion

⅔ oz (20 g) unsalted butter

1 7-oz (200 g) round piece of veal sweetbread

0.4 cup (10 cl) dry white wine

FOR THE ARTICHOKES AND SALMON

4 artichoke bottoms (fresh or frozen)

2 or 3 slices of smoked salmon (about 5 oz - 150 g)

0.6 cup (15 cl) heavy cream

TO SERVE

Salmon caviar, to taste

3 ½ tbsp (5 cl) heavy cream for decorating

1 tbsp yuzu juice

A few sprigs of chervil

Rye bread crisps or artichoke crisps (optional)

Salt, white Kampot pepper

1 day ahead

THE BRAISED VEAL SWEETBREADS

Peel and slice the carrot and onion.

In a saucepan, sweat the carrot and onion in butter. Add the sweetbreads, then the white wine. Cook for 5 minutes on each side. Drain the sweetbreads and peel off their skin while they are still warm. Wrap them tightly in plastic wrap, giving them an even round shape. Let cool and refrigerate for 24 hours.

The next day

THE ARTICHOKES AND SALMON

Cook the artichoke bottoms in boiling salted water for 40 to 45 minutes. If they are very fresh, keep a few leaves for final decoration.

Using a round cutter, cut the artichoke bottoms into neat round slices, then each slice into 2 disks. Set the trimmings aside.

Using the same cutter, cut out 8 disks of salmon and 8 disks of sweetbread. Set the trimmings aside.

Chop all the trimmings — artichoke, salmon, and sweetbreads — together.

Whisk the heavy cream in a salad bowl until light and stiff. Stir in all the trimmings to make rillettes. Season with salt and freshly ground pepper.

TO SERVE

Mount the dish with the help of the cutter: lay 1 artichoke slice on each plate. Cover with 1 slice of sweetbread, then with 1 slice of salmon. Spread an even layer of rillettes on top. Repeat once in order to get two layers of each ingredient, with the salmon on top.

Add a few artichoke leaves (if using) and dot them with salmon caviar.

Add a few drops of whipped cream mixed with the yuzu juice on each plate. Decorate with chervil (and artichoke crisps if you have some). Season with freshly ground white Kampot pepper.

Vegetable Tatin
with Sainte-Maure Cheese

PREPARATION TIME
30 MINUTES

COOKING TIME
8 MINUTES

SERVES 4

FOR THE VEGETABLE TATIN

8 cherry tomatoes

Olive oil

4 young carrots with their leaves on

2 yellow beets

4 turnips

Butter for the rings

Sugar (preferably muscovado)

4 disks of puff pastry, a bit larger than your rings

FOR THE DRESSING

½ oz (15 g) honey

Balsamic vinegar

Olive oil

TO SERVE

Mixed young salad greens (mesclun)

1.8 oz (50 g) semi-dry Sainte-Maure goat cheese

Fleur de sel

Salt, ma khaen berries

THE VEGETABLE TATIN

Preheat the oven to 350 °F (180 °C, gas mark 6).

In a frying pan, cook the cherry tomatoes with a dash of olive oil to evaporate their juice and avoid soaking the crust later. Remove the stems from 4 of the tomatoes, which will not be visible in the final result.

Peel the carrots, beets and turnips.

Butter 4 steel rings, 3.5 inches (9 cm) in diameter, trim the vegetables to the size and shape of the rings, and arrange them inside, pressing them closely together. Season with freshly ground ma khaen berries and 1 pinch of sugar.

Cover the vegetables with the puff pastry, tucking it neatly inside the rings. Prick the pastry all over with a fork.

Bake for 7 to 8 minutes. Turn over while warm to unmold the Tatins.

THE DRESSING

Mix the slightly warmed honey with a few drops of balsamic vinegar, then add the olive oil in a thin stream, whisking vigorously.

TO SERVE

Alongside the tatins, serve a mesclun salad with a few slivers of Sainte-Maure cheese tossed in. Season with a little fleur de sel and freshly ground ma khaen berries.

Green Asparagus Risotto,
Serrano Ham, Quail's Eggs, Truffle

PREPARATION TIME
20 MINUTES

COOKING TIME
6 MINUTES

SERVES 4

FOR THE ASPARAGUS

12 large green asparagus

0.4 cup (10 cl) heavy cream

2 tbsp olive oil

0.6 cup (15 cl) chicken stock

*2.5 oz (70 g) grated
Parmesan cheese*

TO SERVE

*0.4 oz (12 g) black truffle
(preferably Tuber melanosporum)*

12 thin slices of serrano ham

8 quail's eggs

Salt, black Sarawak pepper

THE ASPARAGUS

Trim off the fibrous part of all the asparagus stalks. Set aside 4 of the tips.

Cook 8 whole asparagus in boiling salted water. Drain.

Finely dice the cooked asparagus in order to obtain an asparagus "risotto".

In a bowl, whip the cream to soft peaks.

Heat the olive oil in a saucepan and add the asparagus "risotto". Stir gently until each small dice of asparagus is coated with oil. Add the warmed chicken stock, just covering the asparagus. Simmer for 5 minutes, stirring constantly. Once the stock has evaporated, stir in the whipped cream, then the grated Parmesan cheese. Season with freshly ground black Sarawak pepper.

TO SERVE

Chop the truffles.

Lay a slice of ham on each plate. In the middle of each slice, drop 2 spoonfuls of asparagus "risotto", 1 spoonful of chopped truffle and 2 raw quail's egg yolks. Fold the ham loosely onto the garnish, purse-like.

Decorate with the sliced raw asparagus tips. Season with freshly ground Sarawak pepper. Do not add salt - there is enough of it in the Parmesan cheese and the chicken stock.

Blue Lobster Ravioli,
White Radish

PREPARATION TIME		COOKING TIME
1 HOUR		15–20 MINUTES

FREEZING TIME
1 HOUR

SERVES 4

FOR THE LOBSTERS

1 carrot

1 onion

Olive oil

0.4 cup (10 cl) dry white wine

Coarse sea salt

2 blue lobsters, 1 lb (450 g) each

FOR THE LOBSTER ROE GRATIN MIX

1 oz (30 g) unsalted butter, softened

⅓ cup (40 g) dry breadcrumbs

FOR THE RAVIOLI

6 oz (175 g) white radish or daikon

FOR THE MALTAISE SAUCE

2 egg yolks

1 stick + 1 tbsp (125 g) clarified butter

The juice of 1 blood orange

FOR THE GLACÉ RADISH

8 small radishes with their leaves on

Olive oil

Sherry vinegar

TO SERVE

Sprigs of chervil

Olive oil

Sherry vinegar

Salt, white Sarawak pepper

THE LOBSTERS

Peel and slice the carrot and onion.

In a large saucepan, sauté the carrot and onion in olive oil. Add the white wine. Mix well, then cover with water. Add coarse salt to taste and season with freshly ground white Sarawak pepper. Bring to a boil. Throw the lobsters into this broth and boil for 5 minutes.

Remove the lobsters from the saucepan. Separate their heads from their tails. Set both aside. Boil the claws in the same stock for 2 more minutes.

Pick out the roe and all the white and brown meat from each lobster, discarding the shell and stomach.

THE LOBSTER ROE GRATIN MIX

In a large bowl, mix the lobster roe, the softened butter and the breadcrumbs. Knead well.

Lay this mixture between two sheets of parchment paper and roll it out to a regular $1/10$ to $1/8$-inch (2.5 to 3 mm) thickness. Freeze for 1 hour.

THE RAVIOLI

Slice the claw and tail meat into 12 chunks about $1/3$-inch (1 cm) thick.

Peel the radish, keeping only the thickest part. Keep the thinner part for another use.

Using a mandolin slicer, cut 24 thin round slices of radish.

Boil some salted water in a saucepan, add the radish slices and cook for 1 minute, keeping them crispy. Drain on absorbent paper (do not refresh them in cold water).

On a baking sheet, lay the 24 radish slices and season them with freshly ground white Sarawak pepper. Lay the 12 lobster slices on half the radish slices and cover with remaining slices. Set aside.

THE MALTAISE SAUCE

In a saucepan, on low heat, beat the egg yolks with a tablespoonful of cold water until doubled in bulk and foamy. Off the heat, whisk in the clarified butter, then the blood orange juice. Keep in a warm place.

THE GLACÉ RADISH

Brush and trim the radish, removing the leaves.

In a saucepan, cook the radish al dente with 1 teaspoonful of olive oil, a few drops of water and a dash of Sherry vinegar. Stir them gently until they're nicely coated with the glaze.

TO SERVE

Use a round cutter to make 12 disks of lobster roe gratin mix.

Lay 1 disk of gratin mix (still frozen) on each ravioli. Put under the broiler for 1 minute until golden and slightly warmed.

Put 3 ravioli on each plate, add the glacé radish. Add a few dots of maltaise sauce and a few sprigs of chervil, then pour a thin stream of olive oil and sherry vinegar over each plate.

Bay Scallops, Duck,
Autumn Sun

PREPARATION TIME	COOKING TIME
50 MINUTES	**10 MINUTES**
STEEPING TIME	REFRIGERATING TIME
30 MINUTES	**1 HOUR**

SERVES 4

FOR THE GIZZARD MAKI ROLLS

*3 oz (80 g) of duck gizzards
preserved in duck fat*

*1 tsp reduced balsamic vinegar
(cream of balsamic)*

2 sheets nori seaweed

FOR THE INFUSED JUS

0.4 cup (10 cl) fish stock

½ stick (50 g) butter

FOR THE REDUCED ORANGE JUICE

The juice of 1 orange

½ tsp sugar

**FOR THE SCALLOPS AND THE
"AUTUMN SUN" GARNISH**

8 bay scallops

1 quince, poached in syrup

2 small fresh figs

1 golden delicious apple

2 dried pears

2 1.4-oz (40 g) slices of raw duck foie gras

*2 oz (60 g) smoked duck
breast (magret fumé)*

Olive oil

TO SERVE

Coarse salt

Salt, sil timur

THE GIZZARD MAKI ROLLS

Chopped the preserved gizzards.

In a large bowl, stir the cream of balsamic into the gizzards until well mixed.

Slightly moisten a sheet of nori seaweed and lay it on a sheet of plastic wrap. Spread the mixture onto the seaweed in a regular layer, leaving a narrow uncovered margin at one of the ends of the sheet. Roll the seaweed tightly around the ingredients. Repeat with the remaining stuffing and the second sheet, then refrigerate for 1 hour.

THE INFUSED JUS

In a saucepan, bring the fish stock to a boil. Take off the heat, add the sil timur, cover and let steep for 30 minutes. Strain.

Boil the stock again, add the butter and whisk vigorously. Do not add salt.

THE REDUCED ORANGE JUICE

In a saucepan, boil down the orange juice and sugar until syrupy.

THE SCALLOPS AND THE "AUTUMN SUN" GARNISH

Preheat the oven to 350 °F (180 °C, gas mark 6).

Clean and trim the scallops: remove all innards and tough side muscle, keeping the muscle attached to the shell. Rinse thoroughly under cold running water.

Cut the quince and figs into quarters. Dice the apple and dried pears.

In a hot, dry pan, sear the quince briefly on both sides.

Cut the foie gras into cubes, dice the duck breast.

Sear the foie gras quickly on both sides in a hot pan. Season with salt and coarsely crushed sil timur.

Arrange the garnish around the scallop muscles in their shells. Add a little olive oil.

Put the scallops on a baking sheet, pour the infused jus over them and bake for 2 to 3 minutes just to sear them quickly.

TO SERVE

Remove the plastic wrap from the maki rolls. Cut the rolls into thin slices.

Lay the scallop shells on a bed of coarse salt. Draw a line of reduced orange juice on one side of the shells and lay the maki slices on it. Season with finely ground sil timur.

Cancale Oysters in Escabeche,
Coriander Seeds

PREPARATION TIME
25 MINUTES

SERVES 4

FOR THE VEGETABLES

1 carrot

1 garlic clove

½ white onion

2 celery sticks

½ fennel bulb

1 tbsp olive oil

½ tsp coriander seeds

1 sprig of thyme

1 tsp black Penja peppercorns

0.4 oz (10 cl) dry white wine

**FOR THE OYSTERS
AND ESCABECHE**

24 Cancale oysters, size n° 3

FOR THE FINISHING TOUCH

½ tsp tarragon leaves

½ tsp fresh chives

*A few leaves of oyster
plant (optional)*

THE VEGETABLES

Peel the carrot and garlic. Finely dice the carrot, white onion, celery and fennel.

In a saucepan, sweat the diced vegetables, garlic, crushed coriander seeds, thyme and freshly ground black Penja pepper in olive oil. Add the white wine, scraping the pan with a wooden spatula in order to deglaze the cooking juices, then boil down by half. Pour into a bowl and set aside.

THE OYSTERS AND ESCABECHE

Shuck the oysters, separate the meat from the bottom shell with the tip of your oyster knife. Gather the oyster water into a bowl and strain it through a fine-meshed strainer.

Pour the oyster water onto the vegetables in the bowl. Keep refrigerated.

TO SERVE

Chop the tarragon and chives.

Shortly before serving, divide the diced vegetables between all the oysters and pour the escabeche juice over them. Sprinkle with chopped tarragon and chives, and add a few leaves of oyster plant, if using.

Smoked Salmon,
Celery and Celery Water

PREPARATION TIME
30 MINUTES

COOKING TIME
1 MINUTE

REFRIGERATING TIME
30 MINUTES

SERVES 4

FOR THE CELERY WATER

1 bunch of celery

1 or 2 leaves gelatin

**FOR THE CELERY ROOT
RÉMOULADE AND
THE DICED APPLE**

¼ head of root celery

1 egg yolk

*⅔ oz (20 g) whole grain mustard
(moutarde de Meaux)*

1.3 tbsp (2 cl) red wine vinegar

0.6 cup (15 cl) peanut oil

1 organic Granny Smith apple

juice of ½ lemon

salt, freshly ground pepper

*4 smoked salmon steaks, cut
from the thickest part of the
fillet, 3 oz (80-90 g) each*

wood sorrel leaves

1 tsp Penja peppercorns in brine

THE CELERY WATER

Trim off the tough parts of the head of celery.
Keep the tender, pale yellow leaves that you may
find in it.

Run the celery sticks through a juicer. Collect the
juice.

Soak the gelatin in a bowl of cold water.

Heat a little celery juice in a saucepan; when it
simmers, take off the heat and add the drained
gelatin. Let it melt.

Pour the liquid onto the remaining celery juice.
Mix well. Refrigerate for 30 minutes.

**THE CELERY ROOT RÉMOULADE
AND DICED APPLE**

Peel the root celery and cut it into fine julienne
(very thin sticks).

Put the egg yolk in a bowl. Add the mustard,
vinegar, salt and pepper. Whisk vigorously.
Gradually add the oil, still whisking. Once the
sauce thickens into mayonnaise, season with salt
and pepper as needed.

TO SERVE

Arrange the celery root rémoulade in the center
of each soup plate, and put the salmon on it.
Scatter oxalis and celery leaves on top. Add the
diced apple.

Whisk the jellied celery water in order to break
the gelatin into pieces. Pour it around the
salmon. Season with the chopped green Penja
peppercorns.

Bluefin Tuna,
Raspberries, Piquillo Peppers

PREPARATION TIME	COOKING TIME
20 MINUTES	1 MINUTE

SERVES 4

FOR THE PIQUILLO COULIS

*4.4 oz (125 g) canned
piquillo peppers*

6 oz (180 g) raspberries

2 tsp white balsamic vinegar

*Espelette pepper (or medium-
hot red chili powder)*

fine salt

**FOR THE BLUEFIN
TUNA TARTARE**

*0.8 lb (400 g) extremely
fresh bluefin tuna meat*

juice of 1 lime

olive oil

fine salt

a few Tasmanian pepper berries

TO SERVE

8 raspberries

1.8 oz (50 g) arugula

a few Tasmanian pepper berries

THE PIQUILLO COULIS

Drain the piquillo peppers and remove any seeds.

Heat them in a pan until lightly colored.

Blend them with the raspberries, the vinegar and a little water until smooth.

Season to taste with some Espelette pepper and fine salt.

THE BLUEFIN TUNA TARTARE

Slice the tuna across the grain, then finely dice it.

Season to taste with the lime juice, olive oil, salt and crushed Tasmanian pepper berries.

TO SERVE

Slice the raspberries.

Lay the tartare in a long straight line onto each plate. Add the sliced raspberries.

Add the piquillo coulis on the side and decorate with a few arugula leaves and some crushed Tasmanian pepper berries.

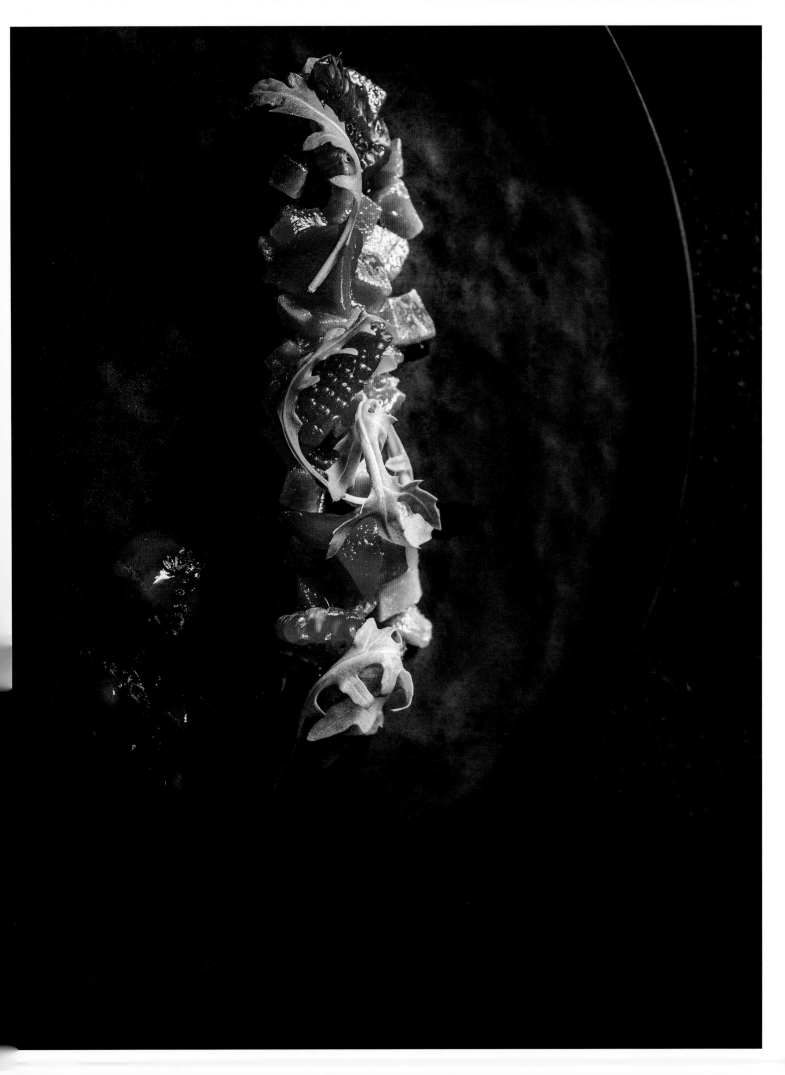

Duck Terrine
with Sake-Infused Dried Pears

PREPARATION TIME	COOKING TIME
50 MINUTES	1 HOUR AND 10 MINUTES

SERVES 4

7 oz (200 g) shallots

3.5 oz (100 g) black trumpet mushrooms

1.4 oz (40 g) butter

1 tbsp sugar

fine salt

FOR THE SAKE-INFUSED DRIED PEARS

0.9 lb (400 g) dried pears

5 tbsp sake

FOR THE MARINADE

3 lb (1,5 kg) duck breast (magret)

3 lb (1,5 kg) pork jowl

10 oz (300 g) cubed duck breast, without fat

1.8 oz (50 g) salt

1 heaping tsp (6 g) sugar

1 heaping tsp (6 g) white Muntok pepper

2 tsp Armagnac

Three days ahead

Peel and quarter the shallots. Clean and trim the black trumpet mushrooms.

Sauté the shallots on medium heat in a saucepan with ⅔ oz (20 g) butter until lightly colored. Sprinkle with the sugar and caramelize on low heat. Cover with water, add salt and continue cooking, uncovered, until the water is completely evaporated.

THE SAKE-INFUSED DRIED PEARS

Put the dried pears in a large bowl. Cover them with boiling water and let them soak for at least 12 hours.

Once the pears are rehydrated, drain and chop them. Put them in a bowl and add the sake. Mix well.

THE MARINADE

Coarsely dice the duck breasts. Put them in a large bowl.

Add the diced pork jowl, diced fatless duck breast, sugar, salt, crushed Muntok pepper and Armagnac, cover and refrigerate for 12 hours.

Two days ahead

THE TERRINE

Preheat the oven to 375 °F (190 °C, gas mark 6).

Grind the marinated meats in a meat grinder fitted with the medium plate, then add the caramelized shallots, black trumpet mushrooms and chopped sake-infused dried pears. Mix well.

Transfer the preparation to a terrine dish, packing it well.

Bake for 20 minutes, then lower the temperature to 250 °F (120 °C, gas mark 4) and continue baking for 40 minutes.

When the terrine is ready, take it out of the oven, let it rest for about 30 minutes, then refrigerate it for 48 hours before eating it.

Salsify and Jerusalem
Artichoke, Pepper Caramel

PREPARATION TIME
45 MINUTES

COOKING TIME
ABOUT 35 MINUTES

SERVES 4

FOR THE PEPPER CARAMEL

½ oz (15 g) acacia honey

1 tsp red Phú Quôc pepper

3 ½ tbsp (5 cl) balsamic vinegar

3 ½ tbsp (5 cl) soy sauce

FOR THE SALSIFY

8 salsify

1 garlic clove

olive oil

3 ½ tbsp (5 cl) spirit vinegar

1 cup chicken stock

FOR THE JERUSALEM ARTICHOKES

8 Jerusalem artichokes

coarse salt

olive oil

oil for deep-frying

TO SERVE

⅔ oz (20 g) butter

salt

a few leaves of garden cress or purslane

THE PEPPER CARAMEL

Heat the honey in a saucepan until foamy.

Add the crushed Phú Quôc pepper, then the balsamic vinegar. Stir with a wooden spatula, scraping the bottom of the pan in order to dissolve the honey. Boil down by half, then add the soy sauce. Set aside.

THE SALSIFY

Peel the salsify and halve them crosswise. Peel the garlic.

In a sauté pan, sauté the salsify and garlic in olive oil.

Add the white vinegar, stir with a wooden spatula, scraping the bottom of the pan to dissolve the juices. Add the chicken stock to barely cover the salsify.

Boil gently for 20 minutes until the salsify are very tender. Set aside.

THE JERUSALEM ARTICHOKES

Wash the Jerusalem artichokes and scrub them with coarse salt. Cut 6 of them into ⅕-inch thick slices.

In a sauté pan, sauté the artichoke slices in olive oil, keeping them crunchy.

Thinly slice the remaining Jerusalem artichokes using a mandolin slicer or a potato peeler. Lay them on absorbent paper.

Heat the oil for frying to 320 °F (160 °C) and fry the artichoke slices until golden. Carefully lift them out of the oil with a slotted spoon and drain them on absorbent paper.

TO SERVE

In a sauté pan, sauté the salsify in olive oil. When they are golden, add the butter and the crunchy salsify slices.

Season the artichoke chips at the last moment. Arrange the vegetables on the plates and add a teaspoonful of pepper caramel. Decorate with a few leaves of garden cress or purslane.

Sweet-and-Sour Turnip, Spider Crab Meat
in Ponzu Dressing

PREPARATION TIME
30 MINUTES

COOKING TIME
6 MINUTES ENVIRON

MARINATING TIME
24 HOURS

SERVES 4

FOR THE MARINATED TURNIP CARPACCIO

1 small daikon radish

½ garlic clove

1 tbsp water

1 tbsp white vinegar

1 sprig of rosemary

Espelette pepper to taste

FOR THE PONZU DRESSING

1 large organic lime (to obtain 3 ½ tbsp (5 cl) juice + the grated zest)

3 ½ tbsp (5 cl) orange juice

4 tsp (2 cl) grapefruit juice

1 heaping tsp (10 g) acacia honey

½ tsp sanshô berries

A few drops of soy sauce

sesame oil to taste

TO SEASON THE SPIDER CRAB

7 oz (200 g) spider crab meat

0.8 oz (25 g) mayonnaise

3 ½ tbsp (5 cl) lime juice

a few blades of chives

TO SERVE

wood sorrel leaves

a few sanshô berries

1 day ahead

THE MARINATED TURNIP CARPACCIO

Peel the turnip, slice it very finely, preferably with a mandolin slicer.

Lay the slices in a deep dish. Peel and squash the garlic.

In a small saucepan, bring the water and vinegar to a boil with the garlic, rosemary and Espelette pepper.

Take off the heat and strain the liquid through a fine-meshed sieve onto the turnip slices. Cover carefully with plastic wrap and refrigerate for 24 hours.

The next day

THE PONZU DRESSING

Grate the lime zest, squeeze the lime. Pour the lime juice into a saucepan, add the other citrus juices and bring to a boil. Reduce by half. Set aside.

In a saucepan, heat the honey with the crushed sanshô berries until the honey darkens slightly. Deglaze with the citrus juice and reduce slightly. Off the heat, add the soy sauce and some sesame oil to taste.

SEASONING THE SPIDER CRAB

Season the crab with the mayonnaise, the lime juice and grated lime zest, and the chopped chives.

TO SERVE

Remove the turnip slices from the marinade and drain them.

Lay 1 tablespoonful of seasoned spider crab meat in the middle of each plate.

Cover with turnip slices in a rosette shape.

Season with the ponzu dressing, and decorate with wood sorrel leaves and crushed sanshô berries.

Seared Foie Gras
in Aromatic Broth

PREPARATION TIME
30 MINUTES

COOKING TIME
ABOUT 4 MINUTES

REFRIGERATING TIME
30 MINUTES

SERVES 4

FOR THE MAKI ROLLS

*1 romaine lettuce
(about 3 or 4 leaves)*

1 sand carrot

5 mint leaves

1 tsp olive oil

juice of ½ lemon

FOR THE DUCK BROTH

1 carrot

1 scallion

1 stick celery

1 cup duck stock

2 tbsp soy sauce

1 tbsp Batak berries

*4 foie gras steaks,
about 2 oz (60 g) each*

THE MAKI ROLLS

Blanch the romaine lettuce leaves in boiling salted water for a few seconds. Drain well and set aside on absorbent paper.

Peel the carrots. Cut one of them into fine strips (julienne). Chop the mint leaves.

In a small bowl, mix the carrot julienne, olive oil, lemon juice and chopped mint.

Lay a sheet of plastic film on your counter top. Spread the romaine leaves on them. Put the carrot julienne in the middle, in a line. Wrap the carrot tightly in the lettuce leaves, making a roll.

Refrigerate for 30 minutes.

THE DUCK BROTH

Cut the second carrot into small triangles. Chop the scallion and finely dice the celery stick.

In a saucepan, boil down the duck stock (which should be on the strong side). Add the soy sauce. Off the heat, add the Batak berries, and cover to let them steep. Set aside.

TO SERVE

Preheat the oven to 350 °F (180 °C, gas mark 6).

Make the maki rolls: cut the lettuce roll into 0.8-inch (2 cm) slices.

Sear the foie gras steaks in a very hot nonstick pan until colored on each side.

Drain the foie gras steaks on absorbent paper, then put them in the oven for 1 or 2 minutes to complete their cooking.

In each soup plate, arrange the carrot triangles, the chopped scallion and the diced celery, then add the foie gras, cut into chunks. Bring the plates to the table.

Pour the hot broth into a teapot and pour it into the plates in front of your guests. The maki may be served on the side, on a small plate.

Lobster Salad, Soba Noodles
and Seared Avocado

PREPARATION TIME
35 MINUTES

COOKING TIME
40 MINUTES

SERVES 4

2 lobsters

FOR THE LOBSTER JUS

2 shallots

1 stick celery

¼ head of root celery

3 tbsp olive oil

1 tsp tomato puree

3 tbsp white wine

½ tbsp cognac or brandy

FOR THE SOBA NOODLES

3.5 oz (100 g) soba noodles

1 carrot

**FOR THE VINAIGRETTE
DRESSING**

2 tbsp olive oil

2 tbsp sesame oil

*½ organic lime (juice
and grated zest)*

1 tbsp soy sauce

*white Belém pepper
(5 turns of the pepper mill)*

TO SERVE

2 ripe avocados

a few young sprigs of mint

COOKING THE LOBSTERS

Pull out the claws from the lobsters, then separate the heads from the tails.

In a large pan of boiling water, cook the lobster claws for 5 to 6 minutes. While they're still hot, crack the claws, remove the gristle and pick out all the meat. Set aside.

Boil the lobster tails in the same pan for 2 to 3 minutes. Pick out the meat while the tails are still hot. Set aside.

THE LOBSTER JUS

Finely chop the lobster heads.

Peel the shallot and chop it finely. Cut the root celery into chunks.

In a large pan, sauté the lobster heads in olive oil until slightly colored.

Add the chopped shallot, the celery stick and root celery chunks, and sweat them for a few minutes. Add the tomato puree. Mix well, add the white wine and brandy, and deglaze, scraping the bottom of the pan with a wooden spatula to dissolve the juices. Add water to barely cover.

Boil down for about 20 minutes. Strain the broth through a fine-meshed strainer.

Pour the broth in a saucepan and boil it down until thick and syrupy.

THE SOBA NOODLES AND CARROT

Boil some water in a large saucepan, add salt, and boil the soba noodles for about 8 minutes (or according to the instructions on the package).

Drain them in a colander and pour some cold water over them to stop the cooking and refresh them. Drain well.

Peel the carrot; cut it into thin strips (julienne).

THE VINAIGRETTE DRESSING

In a bowl, using a hand mixer, beat the olive oil, sesame oil, lemon juice, soy sauce and freshly ground white Belém pepper. Add the reduced lobster jus. Mix well.

TO SERVE

Slice the lobster tails. Remove all the innards with a toothpick.

Shortly before serving, peel and quarter the avocados.

Heat a griddle and sear the avocado pieces, coloring them slightly.

Season the soba noodles with the vinaigrette dressing.

Divide the noodles between each plate, and add the carrot julienne. Arrange the lobster slices and claws, then the grilled avocados. Decorate with young mint sprigs and finish the dish with a few grains of white Belém pepper.

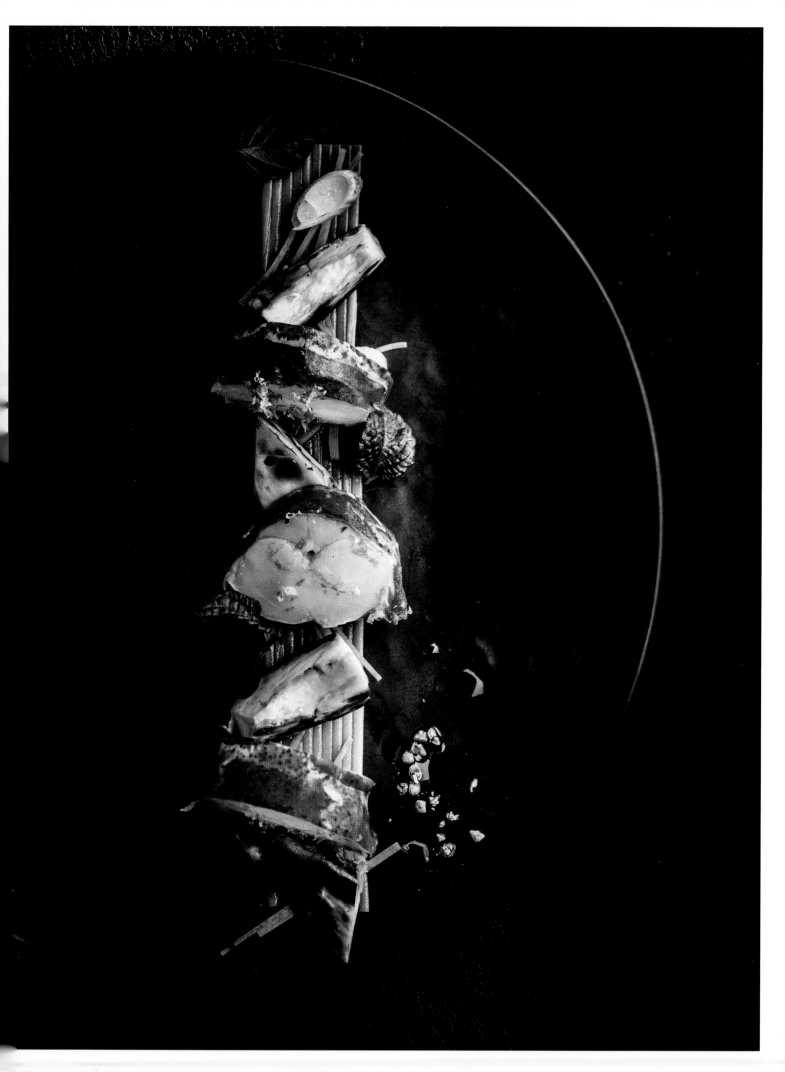

MAIN DISHES

SQUAB, FIGS AND PASTILLA 238

ROAST LAMB, EGGPLANT CAVIAR,
FENNEL BULB AND COFFEE CARAMEL 242

BEEF ROASTED ON THE BONE,
HEIRLOOM TOMATOES AND CECINA 244

FILET MIGNON OF VEAL, VEAL SWEETBREAD
CANNELLONI, MUSHROOMS 246

GÉLINE DE TOURAINE CHICKEN COOKED
IN VOUVRAY "VIN JAUNE", WALNUTS
AND SAINTE-MAURE GOAT CHEESE 248

ROASTED TURBOT, KURI SQUASH GNOCCHI,
PARSNIP MOUSSELINE 250

SEARED SEA BASS CUTLETS, STUFFED ZUCCHINI
FLOWER WITH SQUID, BÉARYONNAISE SAUCE 254

PIKE PERCH, ANDOUILLETTE CHUTNEY 256

CUTTLEFISH AND CELERY ROOT TAGLIATELLE 258

LAMB SHOULDER GRILLED ON VINE BRANCHES,
TIMIZ PEPPER JUS 260

VEAL GRENADINS, TAJINE-STYLE 262

MUSHROOM RAVIOLI, PIG'S FEET, BLACK TRUFFLES
AND FOAMY BROTH 264

FILLET OF ROE DEER, SALSIFY ROOT AND QUINCE 266

PIKE PERCH, GRILLED CARROTS
AND BROCCOLI, SWEET POTATOES 268

Squab,
Figs and Pastilla

PREPARATION TIME	COOKING TIME
45 MINUTES	**25–30 MINUTES**

SERVES 4

FOR THE SQUABS AND THEIR STUFFING

2 squabs (young pigeons, preferably from Racan), 1 lb (500 g) each. You should get 4 legs, 4 fillets, 2 livers and 2 hearts.

1 shallot

⅓ oz (10 g) butter

1.8 oz (50 g) foie gras terrine

1.8 oz (50 g) pig's caul

FOR THE 'PASTILLA'

3.5 oz (100 g) carrots

3.5 oz (100 g) turnips

5 oz (150 g) zucchini

2 fresh figs

0.4 cup (10 cl) olive oil

Allspice, to taste

9 brik leaves

⅔ oz (20 g) butter

Confectioners' sugar

**FOR THE GARNISH
AND THE FIG CAVIAR**

1 quince, poached in syrup

4 fresh figs

olive oil

fleur de sel

⅓ oz (10 g) butter

FOR THE SAUCE

0.4 cup (10 cl) orange juice

1 tsp acacia honey

1 pinch sugar

0.4 cup (10 cl) reduced chicken stock (or jus)

balsamic vinegar

salt, cinnamon berries

THE STUFFED SQUAB LEGS

Remove the thigh bone from each squab leg.

Peel and finely chop the shallot.

Sweat the shallot in butter in a frying pan. Add the squab livers and hearts and sauté them until stiff but still pink inside. Set aside on a plate.

Once they are cold, cut the foie gras into small pieces and lay it on the heart and liver, then mash together with a fork: this is the stuffing. Season it with salt and pepper.

Stuff the squab thighs with the stuffing. Wrap each leg in a piece of caul, shaping them as nicely as you can. Refrigerate.

THE 'PASTILLA'

Preheat the oven to 300 °F (150 °C, gas mark 5).

Peel the carrots, scrub the turnips. Finely dice the carrots, turnips, zucchini and figs.

In a saucepan, sweat the diced carrots and turnips in olive oil. When they are almost tender, add the zucchini which have a shorter cooking time and give a smoother texture. Keep sweating on low to medium heat. When all the vegetables are tender, take off the heat and season with 1 pinch of allspice. Add the diced figs. Set aside.

Lay 3 brik leaves on top of each other, brushing each sheet with melted butter and sprinkling it with allspice and confectioners sugar before adding the next one. Repeat with the 6 remaining brik leaves. You should obtain 3 large disks.

Cut out 4 rectangles about 1.6 inch x 4.5 inch from each one of these disks.

Lay the 12 rectangles on a baking sheet lined with parchment paper, and bake them until they are golden and crispy.

THE GARNISH AND THE FIG CAVIAR

Cut the quince into 8 wedges. Halve the figs and scoop out their pulp.

Mash the fig pulp with a fork, and season it with 1 pinch of crushed cinnamon berries, a little olive oil and fleur de sel. Set aside.

In a pan, sear the quince wedges in butter on both sides. Set aside.

THE SQUABS AND THEIR SAUCE

Preheat the oven to 350 °F (180 °C, gas mark 6).

Put the stuffed squab thighs in a Dutch oven, and bake for 4 minutes. Remove the vessel from the oven, add the fillets and bake for 4 minutes. Set the fillets and thighs aside on a plate.

Pour the orange juice, honey and sugar into the Dutch oven and scrape the bottom with a wooden spatula to dissolve the juices. Boil down slightly, add the chicken jus and a dash of balsamic vinegar. Boil down again. Correct the seasoning with salt and crushed cinnamon berries. Steep for 2 minutes, then strain.

TO SERVE

Divide the warm vegetable compote between the 'pastilla' sheets. Handle the pastilla carefully.

On each plate, put 1 squab fillet, 2 quince wedges, and 1 spoonful of fig caviar. Put 1 stuffed thigh on the fig caviar. Add the sauce and season with cinnamon berries, crushed medium-fine.

Roasted Lamb,
Eggplant Caviar, Fennel and Coffee Caramel

PREPARATION TIME
35 MINUTES

COOKING TIME
40–45 MINUTES

REFRIGERATING TIME
24 HOURS

SERVES 4

TO PREPARE 1 DAY AHEAD

FOR THE LAMB SWEETBREADS

3.5 oz (100 g) lamb sweetbreads

½ carrot

½ onion

⅔ oz (20 g) butter

0.4 cup (10 cl) dry white wine

FOR THE SMOKED EGGPLANT CAVIAR AND THE BABY EGGPLANTS

2 eggplants

4 baby eggplants

olive oil

1 tsp smoked olive oil

FOR THE COFFEE CARAMEL

¼ cup (6 cl) espresso coffee

2 tbsp sunflower honey

1.3 tbsp (2 cl) liquid chicory extract

FOR THE RACK OF LAMB AND THE BABY FENNEL BULBS

1 rack of lamb of 8 ribs
(trimmings included)

1.3 tbsp (2 cl) liquid chicory extract

0.4 cup (10 cl) olive oil

4 baby fennel bulbs

0.2 cup (5 cl) dry white wine

fleur de sel, timiz pepper

THE LAMB SWEETBREADS

Peel and slice the carrot and onion. Sweat them in butter in a saucepan.

Add the lamb sweetbreads, then the white wine. Boil for 2 minutes.

Drain the sweetbreads and peel them while still warm. Wrap them tightly in plastic wrap, giving them the shape of a ball. Let cool and refrigerate for 24 hours.

The next day

THE SMOKED EGGPLANT CAVIAR

Preheat the oven to 250 °F (120 °C, gas mark 4).

Halve the eggplants and baby eggplants lengthwise. Slit the skin of the baby eggplants with the tip of a knife. Burn them on each side using a blow torch of a gas flame.

On a baking sheet, lay the eggplants and baby eggplants, pour some olive oil over them, and bake the eggplants for 30 minutes and the baby eggplants for 10 minutes.

Scoop out the flesh of the larger eggplants. Season it with the smoked olive oil, and set the eggplant caviar aside.

THE COFFEE CARAMEL

Heat the coffee and honey in a small saucepan until you get a caramel. Boil it down (do not let it burn), then add the chicory extract.

THE RACK OF LAMB

Preheat the oven to 350 °F (180 °C, gas mark 6).

Put the rack of lamb in a Dutch oven. Wrap the rib ends in aluminum foil to protect them from the heat. Rub the meat with the chicory extract. Add a thin drizzle of olive oil and season with the freshly ground timiz pepper. Put the trimmings around the rack of lamb.

Bake for 7 to 8 minutes. After 3 or 4 minutes, add a little water and the baby fennel bulbs. Remove the baby fennel bulbs and the meat. Set aside and keep warm.

Deglaze the pan juices with the white wine, scraping the bottom of the Dutch oven. Whisk in the olive oil to emulsify the jus. Strain, season with pepper.

TO SERVE

Carve the rack of lamb into 8 chops.

Use a paintbrush to draw a line of coffee caramel on each plate. Sprinkle with fleur de sel, then add the lamb chops and pour the jus over them. Add 1 baby eggplant, dot it with 1 tablespoonful of eggplant caviar and the braised lamb sweetbreads. Add 1 baby fennel bulb (you may color it on a plancha before serving). Season with freshly ground timiz pepper.

Beef Roasted on the Bone,
Heirloom Tomatoes and Cecina

PREPARATION TIME	COOKING TIME
35 MINUTES	15–20 MINUTES

SERVES 4

FOR THE TOMATOES

1 lb (500 g) heirloom tomatoes of various colors

½ onion

a few basil leaves

olive oil

FOR THE RIB ROAST

1 large 2-lb (900 g) beef rib roast, preferably of the Maine-Anjou breed. Ask your butcher to give you a marrow bone.

olive oil

fleur de sel

FOR THE GARNISH

7 oz (200 g) potatoes (preferably bintjes)

oil for deep-frying

olive oil

TO SERVE

4 to 8 slices of cecina

Salt, Jamaica berries

THE TOMATO TARTARE AND KETCHUP

Cut about 3.5 oz (100 g) of tomatoes of different colors into regular small dice (brunoise) for the tartare. Cut about 1/2 pound (250 g) of tomatoes of different colors in half or quarters. Set aside about 5 oz (150 g) of them for the 'ketchup'.

Chop the onion. Finely shred the basil leaves.

Sweat the onion in olive oil in a pan. Add the tomatoes which you set aside for the 'ketchup'. Stew on low heat until most of the water has evaporated, then add the basil. Blend with a hand mixer. Season with salt and pepper. Set aside.

THE BEEF RIB ROAST

If you have a marrow bone, cut out the marrow and soak it in salted iced water for about 3 hours.

Preheat the oven to 350 °F (180 °C, gas mark 6).

Sear the rib roast on both sides in olive oil in a hot frying pan. Season with fleur de sel, do not add pepper. Put the rib roast in a baking dish.

Bake for 12 minutes for a rare roast. Remove from the oven and let rest at room temperature.

Cut the bone marrow (if using) into round slices; they should be laid onto the rib roast 1 minute before you take it out of the oven.

THE GARNISH

Peel the potatoes and cut them into tiny French fries, about 1.2 inch (3 cm) long.

Heat the oil to 325 °F (170 °C) in a deep-fryer and fry the potatoes. When they are golden and crispy, drain them on absorbent paper.

In a hot pan, sear the halved or quartered tomatoes in olive oil until lightly colored. Season with salt and pepper.

TO SERVE

Carve the rib roast into slices. Season them with freshly crushed Jamaica berries.

Shape the slices of cecina into cones and fill them with the tiny French fries. If you are using bone marrow, once the rib roast is out of the oven, lift out the marrow slices, season them with salt and tuck them into the French fries.

Arrange the beef slices on the plates (or lay them upon the bone on a serving dish if you wish), add the tomato tartare, the seared tomatoes and the 'ketchup'.

Filet Mignon of Veal,
Veal Sweetbread Cannelloni, Mushrooms

PREPARATION TIME	COOKING TIME
50 MINUTES	25–30 MINUTES

SERVES 4

FOR THE SWEETBREAD CANNELLONI

3.5 oz (100 g) veal sweetbreads (from the throat), cleaned, pared and peeled

1 tbsp flour

2/3 oz (20 g) butter

1 shallot

5 oz (150 g) mushrooms

1/2 oz (15 g) black truffle

Madeira to taste

3 tbsp (5 cl) heavy cream

12 large cannelloni pasta

FOR THE VEAL FILET MIGNON STEAKS

4 thick veal steaks cut from the filet mignon

olive oil

3/4 oz (25 g) butter

0.4 cup (10 cl) heavy cream

FOR THE GARNISH

7 oz (200 g) fresh spinach

olive oil

Salt, grains of Selim

THE VEAL SWEETBREAD CANNELLONI

Roll the sweetbreads in flour; shake them to eliminate excess flour. Heat half the butter in a saucepan and lightly color the sweetbreads on both sides. Chop them finely with a knife.

Peel and finely chop the shallot. Set aside 2 mushroom caps and 8 round slices of black truffles (cut to the cannelloni's diameter) and cut them into confetti with a small round cutter. Chop the remaining truffle and mushrooms.

In a saucepan, sweat the shallot in the remaining butter. Add the chopped mushrooms and cook until completely evaporated. Add 1 dash of Madeira and deglaze the pan, scraping the bottom with a wooden spatula to dissolve the juices. Add the chopped sweetbreads and mix well. Add the cream and the chopped truffle. Season with salt and freshly ground grains of Selim. Set this sweetbread filling aside.

Cook the cannelloni al dente in boiling salted water, then refresh them in cold water. Drain, then lay the cannelloni on a clean tea towel.

Spoon the sweetbread filling into a piping bag and fill the cannelloni. Set them aside in a baking dish with a little water. Season with salt and freshly ground grains of Selim.

THE FILET MIGNON STEAKS AND THEIR SAUCE

Sear the filet mignons in a hot nonstick pan with a little olive oil and 1 tsp butter for 3 to 4 minutes. Set aside.

Pour the cream into the same pan and deglaze, scraping the bottom with a wooden spatula to dissolve the juices. Boil down slightly, then whisk in the remaining butter to thicken the sauce. Season with salt and pepper.

THE GARNISH

Heat a frying pan with a little olive oil, add the spinach, and cook on low heat until wilted. Season with pepper.

Microwave the dish containing the cannelloni and water, uncovered, just to warm them up.

TO SERVE

On each plate, lay a bed of spinach and put the stuffed cannelloni on it. Dot the cannelloni with truffle and mushroom confetti. Add the filet mignons, pour a spoonful of sauce over them, and season with freshly ground grains of Selim.

Géline de Touraine Chicken
Cooked in Vouvray "Vin Jaune", Walnuts and Sainte-Maure Goat Cheese

PREPARATION TIME
45 MINUTES

COOKING TIME
ABOUT 15 MINUTES

SERVES 4

FOR THE VEGETABLES

4 to 8 black salsify roots (depending on their size)

juice of 1 lemon

⅓ oz (10 g) butter

1 tsp sugar

FOR THE STUFFED CHICKEN BREASTS

2 oz (60 g) fresh Sainte-Maure goat cheese

1 oz (30 g) gingerbread (pain d'épices)

⅓ oz (10 g) chervil

1 oz (30 g) shelled walnuts

4 géline de Touraine (or any top-quality farm-raised chicken) breasts, skin on, 5 oz (150 g) each

⅓ oz (10 g) butter

FOR THE VOUVRAY "VIN JAUNE" SAUCE

1 shallot

1 tsp (5 g) butter

0.6 cup (15 cl) sweet Vouvray wine

0.4 cup (10 cl) chicken stock

0.4 cup (10 cl) heavy cream

TO SERVE

shelled walnuts

walnuts preserved in spirit (optional)

whipped cream (optional)

Salt, cubeb pepper

THE VEGETABLES

Scrape the black salsify, then wash them. Cover them with cold water in a vessel and add the lemon juice to keep the salsify from discoloring. Drain.

Sauté them in a frying pan with 2 tbsp water and the butter. When they are tender, glaze them by adding the sugar and basting them constantly with the melted butter and sugar. Set aside.

THE STUFFED CHICKEN BREASTS

Preheat the oven to 325 °F (170 °C, gas mark 5-6).

Finely dice the Sainte-Maure cheese and the gingerbread. Chop the chervil.

In a bowl, mix the diced cheese and gingerbread. Add the chopped walnuts and the chervil. Season with salt and freshly ground cubeb pepper. Mix thoroughly.

Butterfly your chicken breasts, making sure not to cut all the way through. Spoon some stuffing onto each breast and spread it into an even layer. Fold the chicken neatly over the filling.

In a Dutch oven, lay the stuffed chicken breasts, skin side down. Add the butter, salt and pepper. Bake for 7 to 8 minutes, then transfer the stuffed breasts to a plate and cover with plastic wrap in order to let the aroma of the cubeb pepper penetrate into the entire preparation. Do not clean the Dutch oven: you need it to make the sauce.

THE VOUVRAY "VIN JAUNE" SAUCE

Peel the shallot and chop it finely.

Sweat the shallot in butter in the Dutch oven. Add the sweet Vouvray wine and deglaze, scraping the bottom of the vessel with a wooden spatula to dissolve the juices. Boil down by half. Add the chicken stock, then the cream. Reduce to desired consistency. Season with salt and freshly ground cubeb pepper.

TO SERVE

Put one stuffed chicken breast on each plate. Add one salsify and a few shelled walnuts. Pour the Vouvray "vin jaune" sauce over the chicken.

Roasted Turbot,
Kuri Squash Gnocchi,
Parsnip Mousseline

PREPARATION TIME	COOKING TIME
45 MINUTES	1 HOUR AND 30 MINUTES

RESTING TIME
1 HOUR

SERVES 4

FOR THE SMOKED BACON CRISPS

8 slices smoked bacon

The seeds from the red kuri squash

FOR THE PARSNIP CREAM

5 oz (150 g) parsnips

1 tbsp white rice

1 cup (25 cl) milk

0.4 cup (10 cl) heavy cream

⅔ oz (20 g) butter

FOR THE KURI SQUASH GNOCCHI

7 oz (200 g) red kuri squash

6 oz (150 g) bintje or bintje-type potatoes

½ egg

3.5 oz (100 g) all-purpose flour

FOR THE BACON JUS

1.2 oz (35 g) butter

1 oz (30 g) smoked bacon, rind on

0.4 cup (10 cl) dry white wine

0.6 cup (15 cl) veal stock

TO SERVE

4 turbot steaks, skin on

Olive oil

Butter

Fleur de sel

Salt, white Penja pepper

THE SMOKED BACON CRISPS

Preheat the oven to 250 °F (120 °C, gas mark 4).

Line a baking sheet with parchment paper; lay the bacon slices and the squash seeds on it. Bake for about 20 to 30 minutes until bacon is crispy and golden. Take the seeds out of the oven when they are nicely toasted.

THE PARSNIP CREAM

Peel the parsnips.

Cook them in a saucepan with the rice, the milk and a little water just to cover, for about 30 minutes. Drain the parsnips and the rice, and blend them into a purée.

Whisk in the warmed cream and the butter. Mix well. Season with salt and pepper.

THE KURI SQUASH GNOCCHI

Peel the red kuri squash and cut it into wedges.

Cook them in boiling salted water until tender.

In another saucepan, cook the potatoes, unpeeled.

Drain the kuri squash. Peel the potatoes while still warm.

In a saucepan, stir the squash and the peeled potatoes until all their water has evaporated, then mash them finely using a potato masher. Put that puree in a large bowl.

Stir in the egg and half the flour, then gradually add the remaining flour until you get a smooth, unsticky dough. Season with salt and pepper, and let rest for 1 hour.

Roll the gnocchi dough into thin sausage shapes, then cut those into small chunks whose length should be equal to the dough's diameter.

Shape them into balls. Position a dough ball on the curved side of a fork and hold it with your index finger while you roll it over the tines of the fork. Repeat with remaining balls, setting the gnocchi aside on a floured plate as you work, so that they do not stick together.

THE BACON JUS

In a pan, sweat the smoked bacon with a teaspoonful of butter. Add the white wine and deglaze by scraping the juices off the bottom of the pan with a wooden spatula. Add the veal stock and boil down by half. On low heat, whisk in the remaining butter, cut into small pieces, to thicken the jus. Add a pinch of sugar; season with salt and freshly ground Penja pepper.

TO SERVE

Preheat the oven to 350 °F (180 °C, gas mark 6).

Bake the turbot steaks, white skin side up (so that the fish remains juicy), with a little olive oil for 4 to 5 minutes.

Cook the gnocchi in boiling salted water in a large saucepan. Once they rise to the surface, lift them out with a slotted spoon, drain them and roll them in a little butter.

On each plate, arrange the gnocchi and the bacon crisps. Insert some fleur de sel and some freshly ground white Penja pepper underneath the turbot's skin to enhance and develop the pepper's aroma. Lifting the turbot's skin is easy after cooking. Put the turbot steaks on the plates and serve.

Seared Sea Bass Cutlets,
Stuffed Zucchini Flower with Squid, Béaryonnaise Sauce

PREPARATION TIME	COOKING TIME
40 MINUTES	ABOUT 15 MINUTES

SERVES 4

FOR THE STUFFED ZUCCHINI BLOSSOMS

½ onion

2 tomatoes

1 zucchini

1.8 oz (50 g) smoked bacon

Olive oil

4 baby zucchini with the blossoms on

FOR THE BÉARYONNAISE SAUCE

1 shallot

Tarragon

Chervil

2 oz (60 g) butter

2 tsp white vinegar

0.4 cup (10 cl) dry white wine

1 egg yolk

1 tsp strong Dijon mustard

0.6 cup (15 cl) sunflower oil

FOR THE SEA BASS AND SQUID

4 bone-in slices of sea bass, cut
in half to make 8 cutlets

Olive oil

4 small squid, whole (heads on),
cleaned and ready to cook

TO SERVE

Olive oil

Balsamic vinegar

Salt, red Sichuan berries

THE STUFFED ZUCCHINI BLOSSOMS

Peel the onion and chop it finely. Dice the tomatoes, zucchini and smoked bacon.

In a saucepan, sweat the onion in olive oil. Add the diced tomato, zucchini and bacon. Stew gently until evaporated, then season with salt and Sichuan berries.

Let cool, then run the vegetables through a meat grinder fitted with a fine plate.

Remove the pistil from the zucchini blossoms. Using a piping bag or a teaspoon, fill them with the ground vegetables. Set aside at room temperature.

THE BÉARYONNAISE SAUCE

Peel the shallot and chop it finely. Chop the tarragon and chervil.

Melt the butter in a saucepan on low heat. Add the shallot, tarragon, chervil, vinegar and white wine. Boil down by half on medium heat.

In a bowl, whisk the egg yolk with the mustard and salt, while adding the oil drop by drop until you get a thick mayonnaise-like sauce. Whisk in the reduced shallot and herb mixture.

THE SEA BASS AND SQUID

Leave the skin on the sea bass "cutlets". Heat a nonstick pan or griddle and sear the cutlets with a little olive oil, briefly, on both sides. Set aside on a baking sheet.

Cut the heads off the squid and slice the bodies into rings. Pull the rings onto the fruit part of the stuffed zucchini blossoms (see photo).

In a hot nonstick pan, sear the squid-wrapped zucchini and the squid heads for about 3 minutes or until golden.

TO SERVE

Preheat the oven to 350 °F (180 °C, gas mark 6).

Bake the sea bass "cutlets" for 2 to 3 minutes.

On each plate, lay 2 "cutlets" and 1 stuffed zucchini blossom. Add the squid head. Drop a spoonful of béaryonnaise sauce, then pour a thin stream of olive oil and a dash of balsamic vinegar over the plate. Season with crushed red Sichuan berries.

BLACK PHÚ QUỐC PEPPER

Pike Perch,
Andouillette Chutney

PREPARATION TIME
40 MINUTES

COOKING TIME
15 MINUTES

SERVES 4

FOR THE RED WINE SAUCE

1 shallot

1 carrot

0.8 oz (25 g) butter

1.2 cup (30 cl) red wine

0.4 cup (10 cl) veal stock

**FOR THE ANDOUILLETTE
CHUTNEY**

*1.8 oz (50 g) andouillette
(chitterling sausage; not to
be confused with Louisiana
andouille sausage)*

*Sugar (preferably muscovado
or dark brown cane sugar)*

1 tsp balsamic vinegar

FOR THE GARNISH

7 oz (200 g) girolle mushrooms

4 baby leeks

⅔ oz (20 g) butter

**FOR THE BACON-
WRAPPED SALMON
AND THE ANDOUILLETTE**

*4 salmon steaks, bone-
in, 6 oz (180 g) each*

8 thin slices smoked bacon

*4 slices from a large andouillette
for grilling (if possible, get a
large 5A andouillette sausage
from Maison Hardouin)*

Salt, black Phú Quốc pepper

THE RED WINE SAUCE

Peel the shallot and the carrot. Finely chop the
shallot, slice the carrot.

In a saucepan, sweat the shallot and carrot with
1 tsp butter and a little crushed black Phú Quốc
pepper. Add the red wine and boil down by half,
then add the veal stock and whisk in with the
remaining butter. Season with salt and pepper.

THE ANDOUILLETTE CHUTNEY

Finely chop the andouillette sausage.

Brown it in a nonstick pan, adding a pinch of
sugar. When the andouillette is browned, add the
balsamic vinegar and mix until you get a chutney
consistency.

THE GARNISH

Slice the girolle mushrooms.

Cook the baby leeks in a frying pan with 1 tbsp
water and half the butter. Season with salt and
pepper, and set aside.

In the same pan, reheat the girolles with the
remaining butter. Season with salt and pepper,
and set aside.

**THE BACON-WRAPPED SALMON
AND THE ANDOUILLETTE**

Preheat the oven to 325 °F (170 °C, gas mark 5-6).

Put 2 bacon slices side by side and roll them
around a salmon slice; secure with string. Repeat
with remaining bacon and salmon.

Line a baking sheet with parchment paper. Lay the
bacon-wrapped salmon and the andouillette slices
on it. Bake for 3 to 4 minutes.

TO SERVE

When the salmon is ready, remove the strings.

Lay one bacon-wrapped salmon slice on each
plate and put a quenelle of andouillette chutney on
top of it. Add one slice of andouillette, the girolle
mushrooms and one baby leek. Season with a few
dots of red wine sauce and some crushed black
Phú Quốc pepper.

Cuttlefish and Celery Root Tagliatelle

PREPARATION TIME	COOKING TIME
20 MINUTES	35–40 MINUTES
(IF THE CUTTLEFISH HAS ALREADY BEEN CLEANED)	

SERVES 4

FOR THE CELERY AND CUTTLEFISH TAGLIATELLE

3.5 oz (100 g) celery root

2 cuttlefish (if you're buying them already cleaned, ask the fishmonger to give you the mantle plus the tentacles and bones for decoration)

FOR THE SMOKED BACON CREAM

2 slices smoked bacon (about 1.4 oz – 40 g)

Olive oil

0.8 cup (20 cl) heavy cream

1 squid ink sachet

1 egg yolk

TO SERVE

Olive oil

Black rice crisps (optional)

Salt, timur berries

THE CELERY AND CUTTLEFISH TAGLIATELLE

Trim the celery root, removing the fibrous parts. Using a mandolin slicer, cut the celery into thin slices, then into tagliatelle-like strips.

Blanch the celery tagliatelle in boiling salted water, keeping them crunchy. Drain.

Cut the cuttlefish mantle lengthwise into strips of the same width as the celery root tagliatelle.

Blanch them briefly in boiling salted water and drain.

THE BACON CREAM

Sweat the bacon in olive oil in a hot nonstick pan. Add the cream, then take off the heat. Cover, let steep for 30 minutes, then strain.

Pour one third of the infused cream into a bowl and color it with a little squid ink until it is quite black.

Pour the remaining infused cream into a large bowl, add the egg yolk and whisk well. Season with salt and pepper.

TO SERVE

Reheat the celery root tagliatelle in a hot nonstick pan with a little olive oil. Set aside on a plate.

In the same pan, quickly sear the cuttlefish tagliatelle on both sides. Cook the tentacles for a little longer.

Arrange the cuttlefish tagliatelle and the celery root tagliatelle on each plate. Draw a streak of smoked bacon cream, underlined with a streak of black bacon cream.

If you have the cuttlefish bones, clean them and use them as props for the black rice crisps and the cuttlefish tentacles. Season with coarsely crushed timur berries.

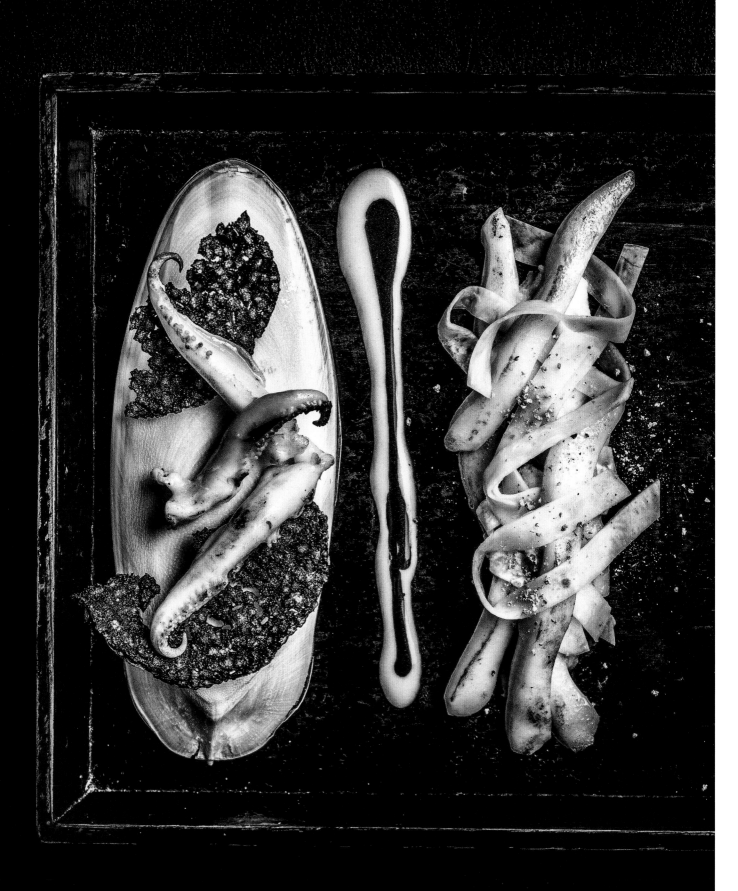

Lamb Shoulder Grilled
on Vine Branches, Timiz Pepper Jus

PREPARATION TIME
45 MINUTES

COOKING TIME
1 HOUR AND 15 MINUTES

RESTING TIME
45 MINUTES

SERVES 4

FOR THE LAMB

3 garlic cloves

*1 lamb shoulder, about 2.65 lb
(1.2 kg), shoulder blade removed*

1 cup (25 cl) olive oil

3 sprigs thyme

2 sprigs rosemary

0.8 cup (20 cl) lamb jus or stock

½ tbsp (2 g) timiz pepper

FOR THE GARNISH

2 eggplants

2 garlic cloves

5 oz (150 g) fingerling potatoes

⅔ oz (20 g) butter

Coarse salt

TO SERVE

½ preserved lemon (in salt)

2 sprigs rosemary

2 sprigs thyme

1 tbsp (5 g) taggiasche olives

Fleur de sel

Timiz pepper

Vine branches

THE LAMB

Preheat the oven to 320 °F (160 °C, gas mark 5-6).

Peel and crush the garlic cloves.

Brown the lamb shoulder in olive oil in a Dutch oven (or cocotte). Season with salt and pepper. Add the garlic, thyme and rosemary.

Pour in a glass of water and deglaze, scraping the bottom of the pan with a wooden spatula to dissolve the juices.

Cover the Dutch oven and put it in the oven. Bake for about 30 minutes.

When the shoulder is done, lift it out of the Dutch oven and let it rest on a rack.

Throw the crushed timiz pepper in the Dutch oven and toast it briefly. Add the lamb jus and deglaze once more. Set aside.

THE GARNISH

Turn the oven temperature down to 300 °F (140 °C, gas mark 4-5).

Trim the eggplants and cut them into large dice. Put them in a large bowl and cover with a thick layer of coarse salt. Leave them to rest for 15 minutes, then rinse them thoroughly under running water and pat them dry with absorbent paper.

Peel the garlic cloves. Chop one finely and crush the other one.

Sauté the eggplants in olive oil in a hot nonstick pan. When they are almost tender, add the chopped garlic. Set aside.

Clean and dry the nonstick pan. Cook the fingerling potatoes in it without adding any fat. When they are almost tender, add some butter and the crushed garlic and continue cooking for about 20 minutes or until well browned and crispy.

TO SERVE

Chop the preserved lemon.

Reheat the lamb shoulder in the Dutch oven for 5 minutes in the oven. Baste it with the jus from the pan and add the preserved lemon on top of the shoulder. Add the rosemary, thyme, and taggiasche olives. Season with fleur de sel and freshly ground timiz pepper.

Take the Dutch oven out of the oven; let the lamb shoulder rest on a rack for 30 minutes.

Reheat the garnish in the oven.

Burn the vine branches in the Dutch oven. Once they turn into embers, put the lamb shoulder on a small rack and place it above the embers, not in direct contact with them. Serve the garnish on the side.

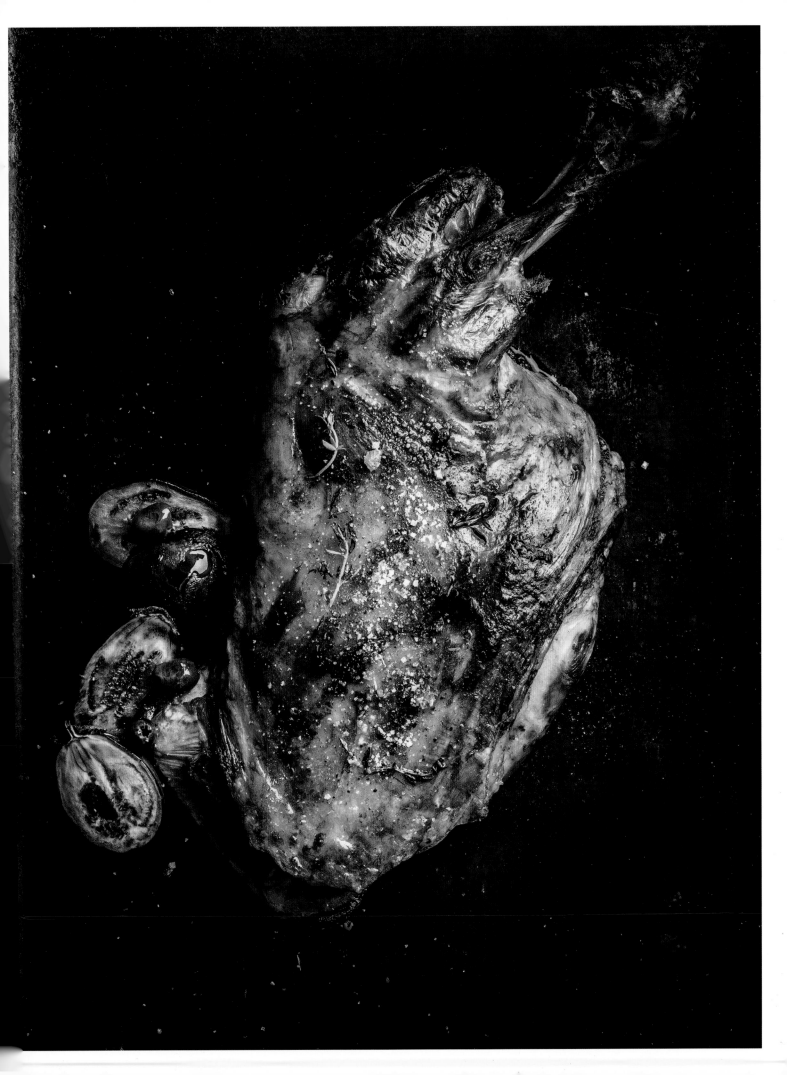

ALEXANDERS (BLACK LOVAGE)

Veal Grenadins,
Tajine-Style

PREPARATION TIME
40 MINUTES

COOKING TIME
55 MINUTES

RESTING TIME
15 MINUTES

SERVES 4

FOR THE GARNISH

0.8 oz (25 g) quinoa

8 baby carrots

4 scallions

3 tbsp olive oil

1 eggplant

1 garlic clove

1 sprig thyme

4 dates

4 apricots

4 blanched almonds

FOR THE VEAL GRENADINS

*0.4 cup (10 cl) veal jus
(concentrated veal stock)*

*4 veal grenadins (thick steaks
cut from the center of the
fillet), 5.6 oz (160 g) each*

1.8 oz (50 g) butter

TO SERVE

0.6 cup (15 cl) olive oil

1 tsp ras el-hanout

2 sprigs coriander

Salt, fleur de sel, Alexanders

THE GARNISH

Preheat the oven to 350 °F (180 °C, gas mark 6).

Measure twice the volume of quinoa in water, pour it into a saucepan and then pour the quinoa into it. Bring to a boil, cover and cook on low heat until all the water is absorbed about 8 to 10 minutes.

Off the heat, let the quinoa rest, still covered, for about 5 minutes to give it a lighter texture.

Scrape the baby carrots. Trim the scallions, keeping only the green part (keep the white part for another use). Cook the baby carrots in boiling salted water for 5 minutes.

Cook the scallion greens in a pan with 2 tbsp olive oil until soft.

Cut off the stalk from the eggplant, then cut the eggplant into large cubes. Lay the eggplant cubes on a large piece of aluminum foil, season with salt and Alexanders, add the olive oil, garlic and thyme. Fold the aluminum into a parcel and put it on a baking sheet.

Bake, lowering the temperature to 280 °F (140 °C, gas mark 4-5), for 30 minutes.

Finely dice the dates, apricots, and almonds.

THE VEAL GRENADINS

Crush 3 tsp Alexanders in a mortar. Bring the veal jus to a boil in a saucepan, add the Alexanders, take off the heat, cover and let steep.

Sear the veal grenadins on each side in a very hot pan until lightly colored. Add the butter, pour the Alexanders-infused veal jus on top of the meat and cook for 3 minutes. Take off the heat and let rest for at least 15 minutes.

TO SERVE

Reheat the quinoa and the diced dates, apricots and almonds in olive oil in a saucepan. Add the ras el-hanout.

Reheat the grenadins in the oven for 5 minutes.

Arrange the quinoa, eggplant, baby carrots and quinoa on each plate. Add the veal grenadins and pour their cooking juices on top. Add a few sprigs of coriander. Season with fleur de sel and crushed Alexanders.

Mushroom Ravioli,
Pig's Feet, Black Truffles and Foamy Broth

PREPARATION TIME
30 MINUTES

COOKING TIME
25–30 MINUTES

SERVES 4

FOR THE MUSHROOM DUXELLES

1.8 lb (800 g) mushrooms, cleaned and washed

½ tsp (1 g) black truffle, preferably Tuber melanosporum

1 white onion

2 cups (50 cl) milk

1.8 oz (50 g) butter

Black Lampong pepper

FOR THE BLACK LAMPONG PEPPER BROTH

1 cup (25 cl) chicken broth

0.4 cup (10 cl) heavy cream

3 tbsp black Lampong peppercorns

FOR THE RAVIOLI

20 squares of ravioli dough (pasta dough)

TO SERVE

3.5 oz (100 g) pig's feet, cooked and boned

2 scallions

THE MUSHROOM DUXELLES

Finely chop the truffle. Peel and chop the onion.

Boil the mushrooms in the milk for 20 minutes in a saucepan. Strain, then chop the mushrooms.

In another saucepan, stew the onion in the butter. Add the chopped mushrooms and half the chopped truffle. Season with salt and freshly ground Lampong pepper. Keep the duxelles refrigerated.

THE BLACK LAMPONG PEPPER BROTH

Bring the chicken broth to a boil in a saucepan and boil down by half. Add the cream and the slightly crushed Lampong peppercorns. Bring to a boil, take off the heat, cover and let steep until lukewarm. Strain.

THE RAVIOLI

Put 1 tsp of very cold mushroom duxelles in the middle of each square of dough. Brush the edges of the square with a little water, then fold one half of the dough over the other half to get a triangular-shaped dumpling. Press edges to seal.

TO SERVE

Finely dice the pig's feet. Chop the scallions.

Boil some water in a saucepan and poach the ravioli in it, a few at a time. When they rise to the surface, lift them out with a slotted spoon. Set them aside in a little hot stock.

Put 5 ravioli in each bowl of soup plate; add the scallions, the remaining chopped truffle, and the diced pig's feet. Emulsify the broth with a hand mixer and pour it over the plates or bowls just before serving.

Fillet of Roe Deer,
Salsify Root and Quince

PREPARATION TIME	COOKING TIME
30 MINUTES	30–40 MINUTES

SERVES 4

FOR THE VEGETABLES

4 salsify roots

*4 quinces, about 10 oz
(300 g) each*

2 ½ tbsp olive oil

1 garlic clove

1 bay leaf

2 tbsp white spirit vinegar

⅔ oz (20 g) butter

7 oz (200 g) spinach leaves

TO SERVE

*4 thick steaks of roe deer fillet (cut
from the loin), 5 oz (145 g) each*

*0.8 cup (20 cl) beef jus
(concentrated broth)*

Red Kampot pepper

THE VEGETABLES

Preheat the oven to 350 °F (180 °C, gas mark 6).

Peel the salsify roots, halve them lengthwise.
Peel the quince.

Wrap each quince in aluminum wrap, put them on
a baking sheet and bake for 20 minutes.

Remove the seeds and core from the quince, then
cut each fruit into 8 matchstick-shaped pieces
(like French fries).

Sauté the salsify roots in olive oil in a sauté pan,
then add the garlic and bay leaf. Add the vinegar,
scraping the bottom of the pan with a wooden
spatula to deglaze the juices. Add water to barely
cover the ingredients.

Melt the butter in a sauté pan, add the spinach
leaves and toss them for about 2 minutes until
wilted.

TO SERVE

Lower the oven temperature to 320 °F (160 °C,
gas mark 5-6).

Heat a griddle or cast iron pan, lightly brown the
quince 'fries' on all sides. Set aside.

On the same griddle, sear the roe deer steaks on
each side with a little oil. Finish their cooking in
the oven for 2 to 3 minutes.

To serve, pour the warm meat jus over them.

Just before serving, season the roe deer steak with
crushed red Kampot pepper.

Pike Perch,
Grilled Carrots and Broccoli, Sweet Potatoes

PREPARATION TIME
45 MINUTES

COOKING TIME
ABOUT 1 HOUR

SERVES 4

FOR THE VEGETABLES

2 sand carrots

½ head of broccoli

FOR THE SMOKED BACON CREAM

1.4 oz (40 g) white onion

⅓ oz (10 g) butter

3.5 oz (100 g) smoked bacon

2 tsp dry white wine

1 cup (25 cl) heavy cream

1 cup (25 cl) chicken stock

FOR THE SWEET POTATO PURÉE

½ pound (250 g) pink-skinned sweet potatoes

1 tsp salt-preserved lemon

0.4 cup (10 cl) olive oil

1 tsp black Malabar peppercorns

TO SERVE

4 pike perch steaks, 4.6 oz (130 g) each

Olive oil

4 thin slivers of lardo di Colonnata

Malabar peppercorns

THE VEGETABLES

Peel the carrots; halve them lengthwise. Separate the broccoli florets from the stem and cut each one in two.

Cook the carrots in boiling salted water, counting about 8 minutes from the moment the water boils.

Cook the broccoli in boiling salted water for about 5-6 minutes, keeping them crunchy.

THE SMOKED BACON CREAM

Peel and slice the onions.

Melt the butter in a very hot sauté pan. Once it has melted, sweat the onions in the butter. They should be translucent, not browned.

Dice the bacon and brown it lightly in the sauté pan. Add the white wine and scrape the bottom of the pan with a wooden spatula to deglaze the juices. Add the cream and stock. Bring to a boil.

Take off the heat, let cool completely, then pour the preparation through a fine-meshed strainer.

THE SWEET POTATO PURÉE

Peel the sweet potatoes and cut them into large pieces. Chop the preserved lemon.

In a hot sauté pan, pour the olive oil and sweat the pieces of sweet potato. Add water to cover, bring to a boil and simmer for 30 minutes.

Drain the sweet potatoes. Blend them into a smooth, very fine purée.

Add the chopped preserved lemon and the grated Malabar pepper to this purée.

TO SERVE

Heat the olive oil in a nonstick pan. Sear the pike perch steaks, skin side down, for about 3 minutes. Turn them over and cook for a few more minutes on low heat. Set aside.

Sauté the carrots and broccoli in the same pan until nicely colored.

Lay the pike perch steaks, vegetables and sweet potato purée on each plate; add the warm smoked bacon cream, then arrange a thin sliver of lardo di Colonnata on top.

Season with a little grated Malabar pepper.

DESSERTS

Tropical Fruit Carpaccio
and Citrus Crumble

PREPARATION TIME		COOKING TIME
35 MINUTES		**ABOUT 2 HOURS**

SERVES 4

FOR THE CRUMBLE TOPPING

1 organic lime

1 organic lemon

1 organic orange

3.5 oz (100 g) all-purpose flour

3.5 oz (100 g) butter

2.8 oz (80 g) ground almonds

*2.3 oz (80 g) sugar, preferably
muscovado, + 1 tsp for
the citrus powder*

**FOR THE CARPACCIO,
AND TO SERVE**

½ pineapple

1 pitaya or dragon fruit

¼ mango

1 orange

1 banana

1 fresh fig

juice of 1 lemon

Batak berries

THE CRUMBLE TOPPING

Preheat the oven to 140 °F (60 °C, gas mark 2).

Using a zesting knife or a vegetable peeler, remove the zest of the lime, lemon and orange.

Spread each type of zest separately onto a baking sheet and bake for about 2 hours or until quite dry, but not colored.

Pulverize each type of zest separately in a blender. Mix each one with 1 tsp sugar.

Raise the oven temperature to 350 °F (180 °C, gas mark 6).

Dice the butter.

Mix the flour and ground almonds in a large bowl. Mix in the butter with your fingertips until you get a regular, coarse crumbly texture.

Spread the topping into 3 separate strips on a baking sheet lined with plastic wrap. Sprinkle each strip with one different citrus zest — about ⅙ oz (5 g) of each. Bake for 3 minutes until crispy.

THE CARPACCIO, AND TO SERVE

Peel all the fruits and cut them according to how you wish to serve the carpaccio.

Mix the lemon juice and some freshly ground Batak berries in a shallow bowl.

Coat with this mixture the side of each piece of fruit that will not be visible, then arrange the fruit according to your taste. Then add the crumble, cut into any shape you wish.

In order to save time and refrigerator space, the carpaccio may be arranged beforehand on a PVC pastry sheet. To serve alongside the fruit trimmings, you may use the remaining dough to make a crumble, and serve with whipped cream flavored with some freshly ground Batak berries

The powdered citrus zests may be made beforehand and kept in airtight containers.

Red Berry
Pavlova

PREPARATION TIME
35 MINUTES

COOKING TIME
2 HOURS AND 10 MINUTES

SERVES 4

FOR THE RED BERRY COULIS

*3.5 oz (100 g) mixed red
and black berries*

1.4 oz (40 g) sugar

0.2 cup (5 cl) water

juice of ½ lemon

FOR THE FRENCH MERINGUE

3 oz (90 g) egg whites

2.8 oz (80 g) caster sugar

2.8 oz (80 g) confectioners' sugar

FOR THE CITRUS ZEST CREAM

1.8 oz (50 g) mascarpone

0.8 cup (20 cl) heavy cream

½ oz (15 g) caster sugar

Grated zest of 1 organic lemon

TO SERVE

7 oz (200 g) berries, red and black

Pink berry

THE RED BERRY COULIS

Stew the berries in a saucepan with the sugar and water for 10 minutes.

Blend, then rub through a fine sieve. Add the lemon juice and mix well.

THE FRENCH MERINGUE

Preheat the oven to 176 °F (80 °C, gas mark 2-3).

Mix the caster sugar and confectioners' sugar. Beat the egg whites to soft peaks. When they become firm, sprinkle with the sugars and beat until firm, smooth and shiny.

Using a spatula, spread the meringue in a regular layer, about 2 to 3 mm thick (about 1/10-inch), on a nonstick baking sheet. Sprinkle with freshly crushed pink berries and bake for 2 hours.

Let cool, keep in a dry place.

THE CITRUS ZEST CREAM

In a bowl, whisk the mascarpone until soft.

In a large bowl, whisk the heavy cream, gradually adding the mascarpone. Add the grated lemon zest and the sugar. Mix until smooth.

TO SERVE

On each plate, drop a dome-shaped tablespoonful of citrus zest cream. Arrange the berries on the cream, then dot the fruit with a little more cream for the broken pieces of meringue to adhere to them. Brush with red fruit coulis to decorate and sprinkle with crushed pink berries.

The lower part of the pavlova may be prepared ahead, but the pieces of meringue should be placed at the very last moment to remain dry and crispy.

Instants of Chocolate,
Sorbet, Ganache,
Cocoa Sponge Cake

PREPARATION TIME		COOKING TIME
1 HOUR		**11 MINUTES**

SERVES 4

FOR THE GANACHE

1.8 oz (50 g) butter

4.4 oz (125 g) heavy cream

7 oz (200 g) dark baking chocolate (in pistoles or broken into small pieces)

FOR THE SORBET

1 cup (25 cl) water

2 oz (60 g) caster sugar

⅔ oz (20 g) cocoa powder

Fleur de sel

2.8 oz dark baking chocolate (in pistoles or broken into small pieces)

FOR THE COCOA SPONGE CAKE

1 egg

⅔ oz (20 g) caster sugar

⅓ oz (10 g) ground almonds

⅙ oz (5 g) flour

⅙ oz (5 g) powdered cocoa

Grated zest of 1 organic orange

FOR THE COFFEE CARAMEL

0.3 cup (7 cl) made espresso coffee

1 tbsp sunflower honey

1.4 tbsp (2 cl) liquid chicory extract

FOR THE NOUGATINE SHEETS

2.8 oz (80 g) blanched, chopped almonds

2.8 oz (80 g) glucose

3.5 oz (100 g) caster sugar

TO SERVE

1 orange

dark chocolate shavings

Voatsiperifery pepper

THE GANACHE

Cut the butter into small dice.

Bring the heavy cream to a boil in a saucepan.

When it boils, add the chocolate and stir until completely dissolved. Stir in the butter and season with freshly ground voatsiperifery pepper. Stir. Pour into a square or rectangular dish, and set aside.

THE SORBET

Bring the water to a boil in a saucepan. Add the sugar, cocoa and 1 pinch fleur de sel. Stir in the chocolate. Whisk vigorously until smooth. Set aside, let cool, then churn in an ice-cream maker

THE COCOA SPONGE CAKE

Mix all the ingredients.

Pour them into a siphon fitted with 2 gas cartridges. Keep refrigerated.

THE COFFEE CARAMEL

Bring the coffee and honey to a boil in a small saucepan. Boil down the caramel without scorching it, then add the chicory extract.

THE NOUGATINE SHEETS

Preheat the oven to 350 °F (180 °C, gas mark 6).

Cook the glucose and sugar in a saucepan until lightly colored.

Off the heat, stir in the almonds with a spatula.

Using a rolling pin, roll out the nougatine between two sheets of parchment paper (or between two silicone mats). Once the sheet is completely cool, break it into pieces, then blend it to a powder.

Spread the powder on a baking sheet lined with parchment paper.

Bake for 2 minutes. Let cool.

Before baking the nougatine powder, you may use a stencil to shape the sheets as you desire. The nougatine sheets should be kept in an airtight container, in a dry place.

TO SERVE

Fill the glasses with the siphon. Heat the glasses, one by one, in a microwave oven at full power for 1 minute each.

Cut the ganache into squares.

Peel the orange and cut out the segments.

Brush each plate with coffee caramel. On the caramel, lay 1 square of ganache, 1 spoonful of sorbet and 1 piece of cocoa sponge cake. Decorate with orange segments, a few chocolate shavings and 1 sheet of nougatine.

Chocolate Pots-de-Creme,
Grapefruit, Limoncello Jelly

PREPARATION TIME	COOKING TIME
45 MINUTES	ABOUT 40 MINUTES

SERVES 4

FOR THE PRESERVED GRAPEFRUIT ZEST

½ organic grapefruit

1 cup (25 cl) water

2 sugar cubes

FOR THE LIMONCELLO JELLY

½ leaf gelatin

0.4 cup (10 cl) limoncello

FOR THE CHOCOLATE MOUSSE

7 oz (200 g) heavy cream
(at least 30% butterfat)

2 oz (60 g) whole milk

½ oz (15 g) timur berries

3.5 oz (100 g) dark chocolate
(55% pure cocoa)

FOR THE CHOCOLATE STREUSEL

1.8 oz (50 g) dark chocolate
(70% pure cocoa)

1.8 oz (50 g) butter, softened

1.4 oz (40 g) turbinado sugar

1 pinch fleur de sel

1.3 oz (10 g) cocoa powder

2 oz (60 g) flour

TO SERVE

1 ½ grapefruit

8 chocolate shells (optional)

4 tbsp chocolate ice cream (optional)

Timur berries

THE PRESERVED GRAPEFRUIT ZEST

Remove the peel from half a grapefruit with a zesting knife.

Drop the zest in a saucepan of boiling water, then drain. Repeat three times. Set aside.

In the same saucepan, bring the water and sugar to a boil. Cook until the sugar is dissolved. Add the grapefruit zest and let steep until it has absorbed the syrup (a few hours). Drain and set aside.

THE LIMONCELLO JELLY

Soften the gelatin in a bowl of cold water.

Heat the limoncello in a saucepan. Drain and squeeze the gelatin, then dissolve it in the limoncello. Mix well, refrigerate.

THE CHOCOLATE MOUSSE

Beat the cream in a stand mixer until firm and fluffy.

Break the chocolate into small pieces. Bring the milk and timur berries to a boil in a saucepan. Off the heat, add the chocolate and mix gently until quite dissolved and smooth. Add the whipped cream, mix well.

Cover the surface of the ganache with plastic wrap; refrigerate.

THE CHOCOLATE STREUSEL

Preheat the oven to 300 °F (150 °C, gas mark 5). Chop the chocolate, and melt it in a double boiler or in a saucepan set over warm water.

Mix the softened butter, turbinado sugar, fleur de sel, cocoa powder and flour in a large bowl, then beat in the melted chocolate.

Spread the preparation on a baking sheet lined with parchment paper.

Bake for 30 minutes.

TO SERVE

Peel the grapefruit, cut off the segments and cut them into small triangular shapes.

Divide the grapefruit segments, preserved zest and limoncello jelly between four glasses or chocolate shells. Add the chocolate mousse. Season each mousse with 1 crushed timur berry. Crumble the chocolate streusel over the mousse.

This dessert may be served with a scoop of chocolate ice cream.

Passionately Passion Fruit,
White Chocolate

PREPARATION TIME
45 MINUTES

COOKING TIME
ABOUT 10 MINUTES

FREEZING TIME
10 MINUTES

SERVES 4

FOR THE PASSION FRUIT MOUSSE

1 ½ leaf gelatin

0.4 oz (12 g) sugar

1 egg yolk

5 oz (150 g) heavy cream

4.4 oz (125 g) passion fruit pulp

FOR THE TROPICAL FRUIT COMPOTE

½ mango

¼ pineapple

Grated zest of ½ organic lime

1 tsp Tellicherry pepper

FOR THE WHITE CHOCOLATE SHELLS

8 white chocolate half-spherical shells

3.5 oz to 5 oz white chocolate (depending on the molds' size)

TO SERVE

Tellicherry pepper

Mango sorbet (optional)

1 day ahead

THE PASSION FRUIT MOUSSE

Soften the gelatin in a bowl of cold water.

In a large bowl, whisk the sugar and egg yolk until pale and creamy.

Beat the cream in a stand mixer until firm and fluffy.

Boil the passion fruit pulp in a saucepan. Drain and squeeze the gelatin, then dissolve it in the passion fruit pulp.

Pour this preparation onto the egg yolk-sugar mixture; mix well. Fold in the whipped cream. Cover and refrigerate for at least 12 hours.

The next day

THE TROPICAL FRUIT COMPOTE

Peel the mango and pineapple. Cut them into small dice.

Stew them in a saucepan until quite evaporated. Add the grated lime zest and freshly crushed Tellicherry pepper.

THE WHITE CHOCOLATE SHELLS

Melt half the white chocolate in a double boiler.

Divide the melted white chocolate between four half-spherical molds. Move and spin the molds around to spread the chocolate evenly inside them.

When the chocolate is set, turn the molds upside-down on a rack. Freeze for 10 minutes.

Melt the remaining white chocolate in the saucepan.

Pour it, in the same manner as above, into the chocolate molds to consolidate the existing chocolate layer.

Freeze for 10 minutes.

TO SERVE

Take the white chocolate shells out of the freezer and let them rest for a few moments at room temperature to unmold them easily.

Using a round steel cutter, place the tropical fruit compote on the plates. Using a piping bag, fill the white chocolate shells with passion fruit mousse, piping the mousse into balls in the end. Season with crushed Tellicherry pepper.

You may serve with a scoop of mango sorbet.

Floating Island
with a Soft Heart of Red Berries

PREPARATION TIME	COOKING TIME
40 MINUTES	ABOUT 10 MINUTES

FREEZING TIME
40 MINUTES

SERVES 4

FOR THE RED BERRY COULIS

7 oz (200 g) strawberries

7 oz (200 g) raspberries

juice of ½ lime

⅙ oz (5 g) pink berries

FOR THE CUSTARD SAUCE

½ vanilla bean

1 cup (25 cl) whole milk

3 egg yolks

0.8 oz (25 g) caster sugar

FOR THE FLOATING ISLANDS

3 egg whites

1 pinch fine salt

2 oz (60 g) sugar

TO SERVE

4 pink berries

THE RED BERRY COULIS

Blend all the ingredients together. Set ¼ of the coulis aside.

Pour the remaining coulis into half-spherical silicone molds or into an ice cube tray; freeze for 40 minutes.

THE CUSTARD SAUCE

Split the vanilla bean lengthwise and scrape out the seeds.

Bring the milk to a boil in a saucepan with the vanilla bean and seeds.

In a large bowl, whisk the egg yolks and sugar until pale and creamy.

Slowly pour in the hot milk while whisking, until completely mixed.

Pour the preparation into the saucepan and cook on low heat, stirring continuously until the custard thickens and coats the spatula. Immediately take off the heat. Remove the vanilla bean and let cool.

THE FLOATING ISLANDS

Preheat the oven to 212 °F (100 °C, gas mark 3-4).

Beat the egg whites with the pinch of salt. When they start getting firmer, gradually add the sugar, still beating. Beat until firm.

Divide the preparation between 4 cylindrical rings about 2.4 inches in diameter, not filling them completely. Knock their bottoms against the work surface to remove any air bubbles.

Insert one frozen coulis cube into each floating island. Smooth the surface with a spatula or a knife.

Put the rings on a baking sheet and bake for 7 minutes.

Unmold and let cool.

TO SERVE

Divide the custard sauce into 4 bowls.

Gently drop one floating island in the middle of each bowl.

Decorate each floating island with a few cut-up berries, sprinkle with crushed pink berries and add the remaining coulis.

Tonic Mojito

PREPARATION TIME
20 MINUTES

COOKING TIME
ABOUT 5 MINUTES

FREEZING TIME
ABOUT 40 MINUTES

SERVES 4

FOR THE SYRUP

2 cups (50 cl) water

4.5 oz (130 g) caster sugar

½ bunch fresh peppermint

1 tsp passion berries

FOR THE GRANITA

*1 tsp (0.4 cl) Get 27®
(peppermint spirit)*

TO SERVE

2.4 cups (60 cl) sparkling water

0.6 cup (16 cl) gin

A few small peppermint leaves

1 tsp passion berries

THE SYRUP

Bring the water and sugar to a boil in a saucepan. Add the mint and freshly crushed passion berries.

Bring to another boil, take off the heat, cover and let steep until completely cold.

Strain the syrup through a fine sieve. Set aside.

THE GRANITA

Add the Get 27 to the syrup. Pour the mixture into a dish and freeze for about 40 minutes.

Using a fork, scrape the frozen mixture to turn it into ice crystals.

Remove the dish from the deep-freezer.

TO SERVE

Pour 0.6 cup (15 cl) sparkling water and 0.16 cup (4 cl) gin into each bowl. Shape the granita with a soup spoon and drop it at the center of the bowl. Add small peppermint leaves and crushed passion berries.

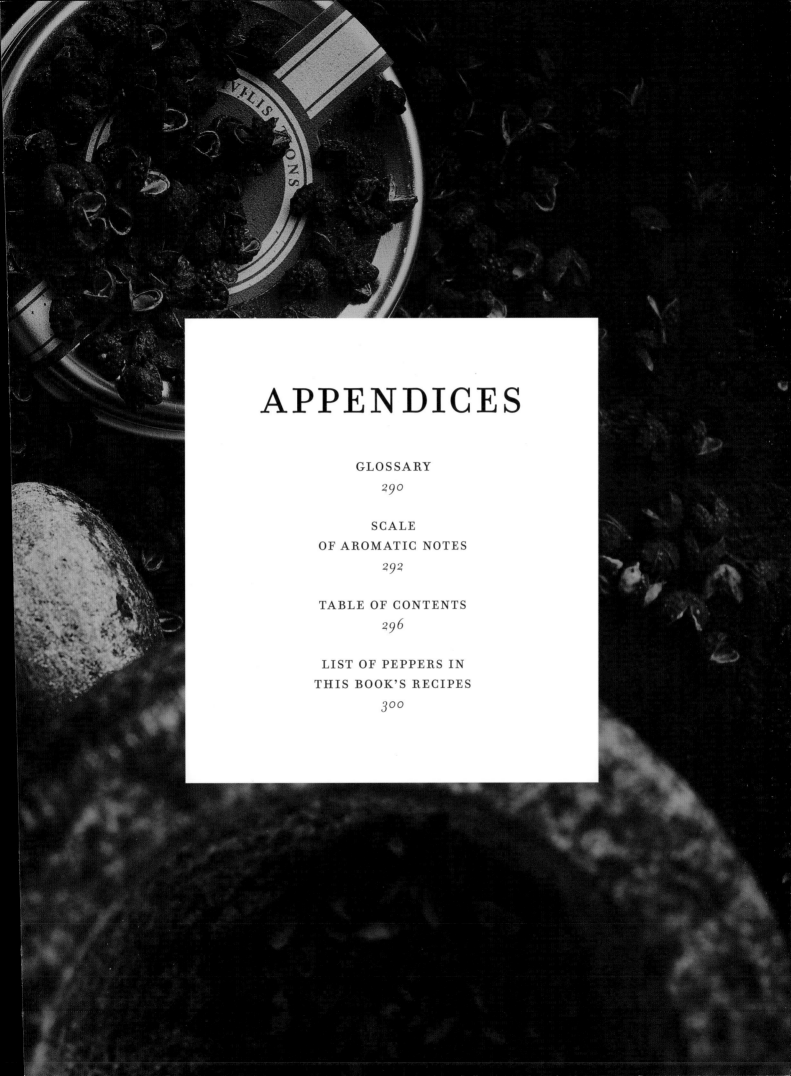

APPENDICES

GLOSSARY

***Anthropic:** having a human origin; caused by Man's intervention. May be said of a landscape, a soil, a relief, etc.

***Berry:** small, fleshy fruit (which generally does not spontaneously open when ripe), containing no pit, but rather one or several seeds.

***Biodiversity:** biological diversity, "within species, between species and between ecosystems" as defined at the United Nations Conference on Environment and Development (1992).

***Fruit:** edible organ of a flowering plant containing one or several seeds. It is formed from the ovary of the flower.

***Seed:** structure that contains and protects the plant embryo. (The reproductive unit in a plant.) It often grows within a fruit, which enables its dissemination.

***PGI (Protected Geographical Indication):** identifies a raw or processed agricultural product of which the quality, reputation or other characteristics are linked to its geographical origin. It was established by a European regulation in 1992. Initially it only included specific food products bearing geographical names and having ties to their geographical origins before it was extended to the wine-making sector in 2009. The indication is associated with a certain expertise. It is not created; it covers an existing production which it protects on national and international levels. Penja white pepper is among one of the first three PGIs of the African continent.

***Pericarp:** the layer of the fruit surrounding the seed or seed bundles in a plant. The pericarp includes the epicarp (skin or peel), the mesocarp (flesh or pulp, edible in some cases) and the endocarp (protective membrane covering the pit).

***Cultivated plant:** a plant whose existence is the result of human techniques. Its growth and reproduction are controlled by humans for various purposes (ornamental uses, food, etc.).

***Endemic plant:** a plant that only grows in a restricted, delineated geographical area (an island, a region, a mountain range, etc.). For example, voatsiperifery is taken from Piper borbonense, a species endemic to the island of Madagascar. Endemism may apply to either plant or animal species.

***Implanted plant:** a plant whose presence is due to Man's intervention. In the case of such introduction by animals, the term is "disseminated plant".

***Native plant:** a plant whose presence within its area of distribution is exclusively due to its own evolutionary processes and not human introduction.

***Wild plant:** a plant that develops and remains in a given area autonomously (including the reproductive process). This term may be applied to indigenous or native species and to implanted species in the process of becoming naturalized or those already naturalized.

Opposite:
A landscape in the Basketo area of the high plains of Ethiopia.

SCALE OF AROMATIC NOTES

	Spice	Balsamic	Animal	Herbaceous	Floral	Vegetal	Fruit	Patisserie	Dairy	Oxidative	Yeasty	Chemical	Empyreuma
PIPERACEAE													
WHITE PENJA PEPPER			●●		●●								●
BLACK PENJA PEPPER		●●					●●						●
GREEN PENJA PEPPER IN BRINE				●	●●								●●
BLACK KAMPOT PEPPER		●●				●●	●						●
RED KAMPOT PEPPER		●●				●●	●						●
WHITE KAMPOT PEPPER					●●		●●●	●					
TELLICHERRY PEPPER				●	●●●		●●						
WHITE NAM BÔ PEPPER	●●●					●●					●		
BLACK NAM BÔ PEPPER		●			●●	●●●							
BLACK LAMPONG PEPPER		●●				●●●							●
WHITE MUNTOK PEPPER			●			●●					●●		
WHITE BELEM PEPPER		●		●●	●							●	
RED PHÚ QUÔC PEPPER		●●	●●●										●
BLACK PHÚ QUÔC PEPPER		●●●								●			●●
BLACK SARAWAK PEPPER		●●	●●●			●							
WHITE SARAWAK PEPPER			●●●	●●		●							
WHITE MALABAR PEPPER			●			●							●●●
BLACK MALABAR PEPPER		●●			●●								
BLACK MADAGASCAR PEPPER					●●●		●●						
GREEN PEPPER DEHYDRATED						●						●●●	●●
GREEN PEPPER ROASTED				●●			●●●						●
GREEN PEPPER FREEZE-DRIED							●●					●●●	
VOATSIPERIFERY PEPPER				●●			●						●●
TIMIZ PEPPER				●●●								●●	●
BLACK MATALE PEPPER	●●				●●●								●
JAVA LONG PEPPER		●●	●●										●
CUBEB PEPPER						●●	●						●●
RED CAMBODIAN LONG PEPPER		●●					●						●●
LIKOUALA PEPPER	●●●						●●						●
ANACARDIACEAE													
PINK BERRY FROM MADAGASCAR					●	●●●	●				●●		
PINK BERRY FROM BRAZIL				●●●		●●●							●
PINK BERRY FROM SOUTH AFRICA				●	●●	●●●							

	Spice	Balsamic	Animal	Herbaceous	Floral	Vegetal	Fruit	Patisserie	Dairy	Oxidative	Yeasty	Chemical	Empyreuma
RUTACEAE													
TIMUR BERRY		•			••		••						
RED SICHUAN BERRY						••	•••						•
GREEN SICHUAN BERRY					••		••				•		
MA KHAEN BERRY				•••			••						•
BATAK BERRY				•	••		••						
SANSHÔ BERRY		••					••					•	
GANSHU BERRY				•		••	•••						
PASSION BERRY					••	•	••						
ZINGIBERACEAE													
KORORIMA				••			•						•••
GRAIN OF PEACE					••	••							•
GREEN CARDAMOM						••	••				•		
BLACK CARDAMOM	••		•										•••
WINTERACEAE													
CHILOE BERRY					•		••						•
TASMANIAN PEPPER		••	•				••						
MYRTACEAE													
ALLSPICE				•		••							••
LAURACEAE													
SIL-TIMUR BERRY				••			••						•
CINNAMON BERRY	•••						•						••
ANNONACEAE													
GRAINS OF SELIM				•		•••							••
APIACEAE													
CORIANDER (SEEDS)				••		•	••						
ALEXANDERS				•		•••							••
CUPRESSACEAE													
JUNIPER BERRY	•		•••			••							
LAMIACEAE													
MONK'S PEPPER	•••					•					••		
XXXX													
MALAM BERRY		•				•••							•

CONTENTS

Chefs' Recipes

Appendices

Opposite:
Dried kororima in its pod, Basketo Country, Ethiopia

LIST OF PEPPERS
IN THIS BOOK'S RECIPES

Erwann de Kerros thanks:

Bénédicte Bortoli, for her generous availability and infinite patience. ...And such talent!

Thierry Nérisson, wine merchant, wine specialist and sommelier, for his enthusiasm and curiosity throughout the pepper tasting process.

Françoise Aubaile, Serge Bahuchet, Marc Jeanson and Marc Herbin of the French National Museum of Natural History, for their historical, ethnological and botanical insight.
And for their generosity in sharing their knowledge.

Guillaume Czerw for his exceptional photo lighting.

Didier Edon and Olivier Arlot, who accepted a gourmet immersion into this world of pepper so readily and so well.

Professor Bernard Roussel for his kindly approach and precious advice, which allowed me a glimpse of an Ethiopia with a fantastic botanical and cultural diversity.

Charlotte Court of La Martinière publishing house, assisted by Gaëlle Demouth, for her perfectionism and also for her tenacity! I now understand how complex the editing profession truly is.

Our clients – fine foods store and restaurant owners –, who place their trust in us, and who, in some cases, have done so from day one. These men and women offer a rich variety of fine products every day, and they are committed to their roles as ambassadors of high-quality products. They need your support!

The team of Terre Exotique, our precious employees and partners who eagerly scrutinize, follow up on, and pass along perfection in pepper.

My father, for having raised me with a taste for travel and a passion for Africa.

Toînette, the good fairy.

Marie, who has accompanied me in this adventure since the very beginning.

Bénédicte Bortoli thanks:

Erwann de Kerros, for his infectious enthusiasm about his experiences with pepper all over the world and for his shared taste for travel and encounters.

Françoise Aubaile, Serge Bahuchet, Marc Jeanson and Marc Herbin of the French National Museum of Natural History in Paris, for the generosity with which they shared their knowledge and for their enthusiasm about this project from its earliest stages.

Thierry Nérisson, for his pepper tasting efforts and his indispensable tasting sheets.

Guillaume Czerw, for having brought out the best in the chefs' recipes to reveal the most attractive profile for each pepper.

Didier Edon and Olivier Arlot, for their creativity and hospitality when welcoming us to the Tours area.

The team of Terre Exotique for their efficient contribution.

Charlotte Court of the La Martinière publishing house, who, with the assistance of Gaëlle Demouth, peppered this work with her expertise!

Photo credits

The photos of the peppers and recipes in this book are the work of Guillaume Czerw.

The photos of landscapes and plants and the stories from *On the Spice Trail* are the property of Terre Exotique (pp. 6, 9, 14, 15, 21, 44, 45, 46, 108-115, 124-135, 201, 202), and certain of them are the work of Patrick de Font-Reaulx (pp. 5, 11, 12, 21, 38-43, 146-155, 291, 294-295)

Texts

Erwann de Kerros

Bénédicte Bortoli

With the collaboration of

Thierry Nérisson, wine merchant, wine specialist
and teacher, for his organoleptic descriptions
of pepper

Marc Jeanson, herbarium manager of the French
National Museum of Natural History in Paris,
for the descriptions of botanical families

Photos: Guillaume Czerw, Terre Exotique
and Patrick de Font-Reaulx

Culinary design: Julie Schwob

Recipes: Olivier Arlot, Didier Edon

Translation into English: Florence and Mark Brutton

Translation of recipes: Sophie Brissaud

English proofreading: Badiane Traductions

With the support of

Terre Exotique

Civilisations et Gastronomie

www.terreexotique.fr